THE
ESSENTIAL
LOTUS

TRANSLATIONS
FROM THE
ASIAN CLASSICS

THE ESSENTIAL LOTUS

Selections from the Lotus Sutra

TRANSLATED BY BURTON WATSON

COLUMBIA UNIVERSITY PRESS

NEW YORK

Columbia University Press
Publishers Since 1893
New York   Chichester, West Sussex
Copyright © 2002 Soka Gakkai
All rights reserved

Library of Congress Cataloging-in-Publication Data

Tripitaka. Sutrapitaka. Saddharmapundarikasutra. English
The essential Lotus : selections from the Lotus Sutra / translated
by Burton Watson.
    p. cm. — (Translations from Asian classics)
  Abridged ed. of: The Lotus Sutra. 1993.
  Includes index.
  ISBN 0–231–12507–0 (pbk.)
  I. Title: Selections from the Lotus Sutra. II. Watson, Burton,
1925–   . III. Title. IV. Series.
BQ2052.E5 W38 2001
294.3'85—dc21
                                                    2001028473

Casebound editions of Columbia University Press books
are printed on permanent and durable acid-free paper.

Printed in the United States of America

p 10 9 8 7 6 5 4 3 2 1

CONTENTS

PREFACE TO THE ABRIDGED EDITION

The Lotus Sutra is a rather prolix and loosely structured text, with some chapters that are repetitious or of minor doctrinal importance and others that were perhaps appended at a later date. The abridged edition of the text presented here attempts to cut through this diffuseness and to focus on the chapters that expound the core ideas of the work and have been most influential in the later development of Buddhist thought.

The abridged edition begins with two lengthy chapters, "Expedient Means" and "Simile and Parable." These constitute the second and third chapters of the Lotus Sutra and set forth the principal doctrines embodied in the first part of the sutra. These doctrines are often referred to as the theoretical or "trace" teachings because they are expounded by the Buddha in his temporal or "trace" manifestation as the historical figure Shakyamuni of ancient India.

In the "Expedient Means" chapter, the Buddha begins by stressing that the wisdom of the Buddhas is "infinitely profound and immeasurable," and that only Buddhas can understand "the true aspect of all phenomena," that is, the true nature of reality. He then states that the Buddhas make their advent in the world for "one great reason" alone, namely, to enable all living beings to awaken and become Buddhas themselves.

He then goes on to explain that, though he had earlier described three vehicles or goals of religious practice, this was no more than an expedient means adopted because his listeners were not yet ready to comprehend the ultimate truth. But now he urges them to set aside these lesser goals or vehicles and instead follow the One Vehicle or Great Vehicle that leads to the attainment of Buddhahood. The chapter stresses that all living beings are endowed with the potential to achieve this objective.

In the third chapter, "Simile and Parable," Shariputra, one of the Buddha's major disciples, responds with joy to his pronouncements. Shariputra had earlier believed that, because he followed the path of the *shravaka* or voice-hearer, he could never hope to attain Buddhahood, but now he realizes that he is fully capable of doing so. The Buddha confirms this by describing how in a future existence Shariputra will become a Buddha with the name Flower Glow.

To further make clear why he had earlier preached the doctrine of the three vehicles and now replaces it with the higher truth of the One Vehicle, the Buddha expounds the famous parable of the burning house. (See the section on The Seven Parables of the Lotus Sutra below.) At the close of the chapter, the Buddha declares that it is faith alone that enables one to respond to the Law and benefit from it, and warns of the dire consequences awaiting those who reject or slander the sutra he is preaching.

The abridged edition then skips to chapter ten, "The Teacher of the Law," in which the Buddha declares that the Lotus Sutra is foremost among all the sutras, and describes how one should preach and pay reverence to it.

This is followed by chapter eleven, entitled "Emergence of the Treasure Tower," which describes how a wonderful jewel-adorned tower miraculously rises out of the earth and hangs suspended in midair. In it is seated a Buddha named Many Treasures, who has come to testify to the truth of the Lotus Sutra. Shakyamuni seats himself beside Many Treasures in the treasure tower and then, in order that his listeners may be on a level with himself, employs his mystic powers to lift the entire assembly up into the air. This marks the beginning of what is known as the Ceremony in the Air, which continues until the close of chapter twenty-two. Shakyamuni calls on the members of the assembly to propagate the Lotus Sutra after his death but warns of the many difficulties they will encounter in doing so.

This is followed by chapter twelve, the "Devadatta" chapter. Devadatta, an evil-minded disciple of Shakyamuni Buddha, comparable to the Judas figure in Christianity, is revealed to have been a friend and teacher of the Buddha in a past life and to be destined to attain Buddhahood himself in a future existence. The chapter also describes a daughter of the dragon king Sagara who, though only a child of eight, has attained the highest level of enlightenment. Earlier Buddhism had generally denied that women could attain Buddhahood, at least while in female form, and one school of thinkers had declared that some people are so inherently evil in nature that they can never hope to gain enlightenment. The Lotus Sutra firmly rejects such assertions. We are to understand that all beings without exception, good or evil, female or male, are equally capable of becoming Buddhas.

The selection then skips to chapter fifteen, "Emerging from the Earth," in which the earth opens and a vast multitude of bodhisattvas appears. Maitreya, speaking on behalf of the entire assembly, asks who these people are. The Buddha replies that they are disciples whom he has been teaching since long ages in the past. Maitreya inquires how Shakyamuni, in the space of one lifetime, could possibly have been able to teach and convert such an astounding number.

Chapter sixteen, "The Life Span of the Thus Come One," answers this question. In it, the Buddha reveals that in fact he first attained enlightenment in an incalculably distant age in the past, and has since then been constantly abiding in the world. This chapter constitutes the heart of the doctrines revealed in the second half of the Lotus Sutra, the essential or "origin" teaching, expounded by the Buddha after he has cast aside his transient role as the historical Shakyamuni and revealed his true, original identity.

At various points in the course of the Lotus Sutra the Buddha, while urging his listeners to embrace and uphold the sutra and propagate it widely in the world after his passing, warns them of the obstacles they will encounter. To strengthen their resolve, in chapter twenty he tells them the story of the Bodhisattva Never Disparaging. A monk who lived many years ago, he was so called because he would bow to every person he met and say, "I have profound reverence for you, I would never dare treat you with disparagement. . . . Because you are all practicing the bodhisattva way and are certain to attain Buddhahood." In other words, he actively testifies to the doctrine expounded earlier in the sutra, that all beings are capable of gaining enlightenment. His listeners, unaware of the truth of his pronouncements and offended by such conduct, curse and abuse him and on occasion attack him with sticks and stones, an offense for which they later suffer for a time in hell. The Buddha then reveals that he himself was this Bodhisattva Never Disparaging in a past existence, and that those who long ago mocked him are now present in the assembly he is addressing.

In chapter twenty-two, "Entrustment," which marks the end of the Ceremony in the Air, the Buddha entrusts the propagation of the Law to the members of the assembly.

The abridged edition concludes with chapter twenty-five, "The Universal Gateway of the Bodhisattva Perceiver of the World's Sounds," so highly venerated in later times that it has come to be regarded as a separate sutra in its own right. It is the most important of the devotional chapters with which the Lotus Sutra concludes and describes the wonderful salvational power extended to all those who call upon his name by the bodhisattva Avalokiteshvara, or the Perceiver of the World's Sounds, known in China as Kuan-yin and in Japan as Kannon. The bodhisattva is said to be capable of assuming thirty-three different guises, matching his form to that of whatever being, male or female, human or nonhuman, solicits his aid. Originally regarded as a male figure, the bodhisattva is frequently depicted in later Chinese and Japanese Buddhist art in female form and is often referred to in English as the Goddess of Mercy.

OUTLINE OF THE CHAPTERS OF THE LOTUS SUTRA OMITTED IN THE ABRIDGED EDITION

1. Introduction: Describes the vast assembly of senior disciples, arhats, bodhisattvas, gods, and human and nonhuman beings gath-

ered on Mount Gridhrakuta or Eagle Peak to listen to the Buddha. The Buddha emits a ray of light from his forehead, a sign that he is about to preach the Lotus Sutra.

2. Expedient Means: In abridged edition.
3. Simile and Parable: In abridged edition.
4. Belief and Understanding: The elder disciples express joy on hearing the One Vehicle teaching of the Buddha and describe their condition through the parable of the rich man and his impoverished son.
5. The Parable of the Medicinal Herbs: The Buddha likens his teaching to a rain that falls equally on all kinds of plants and trees, though they receive and absorb it in different ways depending upon their respective capacities.
6. Bestowal of Prophecy: The Buddha bestows a prophecy of the attainment of Buddhahood on various of his major disciples and describes the kind of Buddha land each will preside over.
7. The Parable of the Phantom City: The Buddha reveals his relationship to his disciples in the remote past, when he was the sixteenth son of a Buddha named Great Universal Wisdom. The chapter concludes with the parable of the phantom city.
8. Prophecy of Enlightenment for Five Hundred Disciples: Further prophecies of the attainment of Buddhahood.
9. Prophecies Conferred on Learners and Adepts: Further prophecies.
10. The Teacher of the Law: In abridged edition.
11. The Emergence of the Treasure Tower: In abridged edition.
12. Devadatta: In abridged edition.
13. Encouraging Devotion: The Buddha assures the nuns that they too will attain enlightenment and describes the persecutions that will be met in the future by those who propagate the Lotus Sutra.
14. Peaceful Practices: Instructions on how to preach the Law or Buddhist Doctrine.
15. Emerging from the Earth: In abridged edition.
16. The Life Span of the Thus Come One: In abridged edition.
17. Distinctions in Benefits: Describes the benefits or blessings gained through devotion to the Lotus Sutra.
18. The Benefits of Responding with Joy: Further descriptions of the benefits to be gained by responding to and propagating the Lotus Sutra.

19. Benefits of the Teacher of the Law: More on the same subject.
20. The Bodhisattva Never Disparaging: In abridged edition.
21. Supernatural Powers of the Thus Come One: The Buddha displays his miraculous powers and calls on his listeners to uphold the Lotus Sutra.
22. Entrustment: In abridged edition.
23. The Former Affairs of the Bodhisattva Medicine King: Description of a bodhisattva named Medicine King, who sacrifices his body as an offering to the Buddha. The chapter has been important in later Buddhist thought and practice because of the passage that states, "If there is a woman who hears this chapter on The Former Affairs of the Bodhisattva Medicine King and is able to accept and uphold it, that will be her last appearance in a woman's body. . . . When her life here on earth comes to an end she will immediately go to the world of Peace and Delight where the Buddha Amitayus dwells . . . and there will be born seated on a jeweled seat in the center of a lotus blossom."
24. The Bodhisattva Wonderful Sound: Description of a bodhisattva who, as a result of his devotion to the Buddha, has acquired the power to appear in any form he wishes in order to propagate the Lotus Sutra.
25. The Universal Gateway of the Bodhisattva Perceiver of the World's Sounds: In abridged edition.
26. Dharani: Describes various *dharani* or spells that will aid and protect those who propagate the Law. Ten daughters of a *rakshasa* demon appear and vow before the Buddha to guard those who accept and uphold the Lotus Sutra.
27. Former Affairs of King Wonderful Adornment: Describes how two sons of a king, hearing the Lotus Sutra, persuade their father, King Wonderful Adornment, to abandon his faith in Brahmanical teachings. The king, his queen, and all their ministers and attendants become followers of the Buddha.
28. Encouragements of the Bodhisattva Universal Worthy: The bodhisattva Universal Worthy vows to protect the Lotus Sutra and all those who embrace and propagate it in the Latter Day of the Law.

THE SEVEN PARABLES OF THE LOTUS SUTRA

The Lotus Sutra is particularly noted for its skillful use of parables, of which there are seven, some employed by the Buddha to illustrate his teachings, others related by members of the assembly. They are as follows:

1. The parable of the burning house and the three carts is expounded by the Buddha in chapter three, "Simile and Parable," which is included in this abridged edition. To explain why, as an expedient means, he earlier preached the doctrine of the three vehicles but now replaces it with the doctrine of the One Vehicle, the Buddha likens the world we live in to an old mansion owned by a rich man (the Buddha) in which fire has broken out. The rich man endeavors to get his sons (living beings) out of the house before they are harmed, but they are so engrossed in their games that they do not heed his warnings. He then promises that if they will go outside the house, he will give them three different kinds of carts to play with. The sons rush out, eager for these gifts, but instead of three carts the father gives each of them a splendid cart of the One Vehicle teaching. As is true of all the parables, the story appears twice, first in the prose section of the chapter and then again in the verse section that follows.

2. The parable of the rich man and his impoverished son. In chapter four, "Belief and Understanding," the senior disciples of Shakyamuni, learning that they are capable of attaining Buddhahood, relate the parable of the rich man (the Buddha) and his impoverished son (themselves) to illustrate their situation. A young son abandons his father and goes off to live many years in another country. Later, reduced to poverty, he comes to the city where his father is now living. The father, who is extremely rich, recognizes his son and takes him into his employ as a menial laborer, but conceals their true relationship in order to avoid alarming him. Gradually he accustoms the son to his presence and to a more elevated way of life until he feels the son is ready to recognize his own abilities and take over the management of his father's wealth. Just so does the Buddha employ various expedient means to gradually enlighten living beings and waken them to the full extent of their capabilities.

These two parables are the most famous and elaborately developed of the seven parables of the Lotus Sutra. The latter is often compared to the parable of the prodigal son in the New Testament.

3. The third parable occupies the whole of chapter five, to which it gives its name, "The Parable of the Medicinal Herbs." The Buddha likens his preaching of the Law to a gentle rain that falls on the various trees, plants, and medicinal herbs of the forest. The rain falls on all equally, but each species receives and absorbs the moisture that is appropriate to its own particular nature and capacity.

4. The fourth parable appears at the end of chapter seven and accounts for the title of the chapter, "The Parable of the Phantom City." The Buddha, explaining why he uses various expedient means to adapt his teachings to the particular capacities of his listeners, compares himself to the leader of a band of travelers who are in search of treasure. Happening on a stretch of unusually difficult road, the travelers grow weary and disheartened and wish to abandon their search. The leader then conjures up a phantom city and urges his companions to enter it and rest. Once they have recovered from their exhaustion, however, he reveals that the city is a mere phantom, whereupon the travelers resume their journey, pressing forward with renewed vigor. The "treasure" they are seeking is of course the attainment of Buddhahood.

5. The parable of the jewel in the robe. In chapter eight, "Prophecy of Enlightenment for Five Hundred Disciples," five hundred arhats, who had earlier supposed that they had attained the highest goal possible for them, are assured that in time they will become Buddhas. To describe their situation, they liken themselves to a man who, having drunk much wine, goes to sleep in the house of a friend. While he is asleep, the friend sews a jewel of priceless worth into the lining of his robe and then departs. When the man awakens, unaware of what has happened, he sets off for another country, where he undergoes great hardship and want. Later he again meets the friend, who tells him of the precious jewel that has all along been sewn into his robe. Too often we suffer needless hardship and content ourselves with a lesser goal because we fail to realize the full extent of our innate capacities.

Note how often in these parables the crux of the problem is not faulty reasoning or wayward behavior, but simply ignorance of the true nature of one's situation or abilities.

6. The jewel in the topknot, the shortest of the seven parables, is

found at the end of chapter fourteen, "Peaceful Practices." The Buddha compares himself to a mighty king and the Lotus Sutra to a precious jewel that he keeps in his topknot. When the soldiers under his command achieve distinction in battle, he rewards them with lands, costly goods, and other spoils of combat. But he does not lightly give away the greatest treasure of all, the jewel in his topknot, reserving it for a warrior who is very "brave and stalwart" and of truly outstanding worth. The Lotus Sutra, we are to understand, is the greatest gift that the Buddha has to bestow.

7. The last of the seven parables, that of the skilled physician and his ailing sons, is found in chapter sixteen, "The Life Span of the Thus Come One," which is included in this abridged edition. Here the Buddha reveals that he attained enlightenment in the far distant past and since then has constantly abided in the world, though he appears at times to pass into extinction and at other times to return.

To explain why he does so, he relates the parable of the skilled physician and his ailing children. While the physician is traveling in another land, his children inadvertently drink some kind of poison that deranges their minds. When the physician returns and learns what has happened, he urges them to drink a medicine that will act as an antidote, but some of the children are so befuddled by the poison that they refuse to do so. The father, realizing that he must resort to some expedient means to induce them to take the medicine, goes off once more to another land and sends back word that he has died. The children are so shocked by grief that they come back to their senses and take the medicine. In like manner does the Buddha shock living beings into a realization of the seriousness of their situation when he appears to leave them and pass into extinction.

TRANSLATOR'S INTRODUCTION

The Lotus Sutra is one of the most important and influential of all the sutras or sacred scriptures of Mahayana Buddhism, revered by almost all branches of the Mahayana teachings, and over many centuries the object of intense veneration among Buddhist believers throughout China, Korea, Japan, and other regions of eastern Asia.

We do not know where or when the Lotus Sutra was composed, or in what language. Probably it was initially formulated in some local dialect of India or Central Asia and then later put into Sanskrit to lend it greater respectability. All we can say for certain about the date of its composition is that it was already in existence by 255 CE, when the first Chinese translation of it was made. It was translated into Chinese several times subsequently, but it is through the version done in 406 by the Central Asian scholar-monk Kumarajiva that it has become widely known and read in China and the other countries within the

Chinese cultural sphere of influence. This version has been universally acknowledged as the most authoritative and felicitous in language, and it is from this version that the present English translation has been made.

In recent years several Sanskrit texts of the Lotus Sutra, titled in Sanskrit *Saddharma-pundarika Sutra* or "The Sutra of the Lotus of the Wonderful Law," have been discovered in Nepal, Central Asia, and Kashmir. Some appear to have been copied in the eleventh century or later, though some may have been copied as early as the fifth or sixth century. These Sanskrit versions of the work differ considerably in places from the Kumarajiva translation, being often more verbose in expression, which suggests that the text Kumarajiva followed was earlier in date, and may in fact have been quite close to the original version.

The Lotus Sutra, as just mentioned, was at an early date translated into Chinese, as well as into Tibetan, and in later centuries into Hsi-hsia, Mongol, Manchu, Korean, and Japanese. In recent years several translations into English and other European languages have appeared; now it is established as an important text of world literature.

EARLY BUDDHISM

Gautama, or Shakyamuni Buddha, the founder of Buddhism, appears to have lived in India sometime around the sixth or fifth century BCE. Though it is difficult to describe his doctrines in detail, Buddhologists customarily accept several formulas as representative of his teachings. Most famous of these are the so-called four noble truths, which are referred to several times in the Lotus Sutra. These teach that (1) all existence in the *saha* world, the world in which we live at present, is marked by suffering; (2) that suffering is caused by craving; (3) that by doing away with craving one can gain release from suffering and reach a state of peace and enlightenment, often called nirvana; (4) that there is a method for achieving this goal, namely, the discipline known as the eightfold path. This is a set of moral principles enjoining one to cultivate right views, right thinking, right speech, right action, right way of life, right endeavor, right mindfulness, and right meditation.

Another doctrine, also touched on in the Lotus Sutra, is that of the twelve-linked chain of causation or dependent origination, which illustrates step by step the causal relationship between ignorance and suffering. The purpose of the doctrine, like that of the four noble truths, is to wake one to the true nature of reality and help one to achieve emancipation from ignorance and suffering.

In order to pursue the kind of strenuous discipline needed to gain such release, it was thought all but imperative that one leave secular life and become a member of the Buddhist Order, which consisted of both monks and nuns. There, free from family entanglements and worldly concerns, one could devote oneself to a life of poverty, celibacy, and religious study and discipline, supported by the alms of the lay community. Lay believers could acquire religious merit by assisting the Order, observing the appropriate rules of moral conduct, and carrying out devotional practices such as paying obeisance at the stupas or memorial towers that housed the relics of the Buddha. But it was thought that they would have to wait until future existences before they could hope to gain full release from suffering.

Buddhism, it should be noted, took over from earlier Indian thought the belief in karma. According to this belief, all a person's moral actions, whether good or bad, produce definite effects in the person's life, though such effects may take some time before manifesting themselves. According to the Indian view, living beings pass through an endless cycle of death and rebirth, and the ill effects of an evil action in one life may not become evident until some future existence; but that they will appear eventually is inescapable. Hence only by striving to do good in one's present existence can one hope to escape even greater suffering in a future life.

Buddhism vehemently denied that there is any individual soul or personal identity that passes over from one existence to the next—to suppose there is is simply to open the way for further craving—but it did accept the idea of rebirth or transmigration, and taught that the circumstances or realm into which a being is reborn are determined by the good or bad acts done by that being in previous existences. This meant, among other things, that one did not necessarily have to struggle for release from suffering within a single lifetime, but could work at the goal of salvation step by step, performing good moral and devotional acts that would insure one of rebirth in more favorable circumstances in the future, and in this way gradually raising one's level of spiritual attainment.

The tenets and practices of the religion I have described above are often referred to as Hinayana Buddhism. But Hinayana, which means "Lesser Vehicle," is a derogatory term, applied to early Buddhism by a group within the religion that called itself Mahayana or the "Great Vehicle" and represented its doctrines as superior to and superseding those of earlier Buddhism. In keeping with the spirit of religious tolerance and mutual understanding that prevails in most quarters today, writers usually try to avoid use of the term "Hinayana," instead referring to the earlier form of Buddhism as "Theravada" or "The Teachings of the Elders," which is the name used by the branch of it that continues in existence today. This is the form of Buddhism that prevails at present in Sri Lanka, Burma, Thailand, Cambodia, and Laos.

The Mahayana movement appears to have begun in India around the first or second century of the Common Era. In part it was probably a reaction against the great emphasis upon monastic life that marked earlier Buddhism and against the arid psychological and metaphysical speculations that characterize much of early Buddhist philosophy. It aimed to open up the religious life to a wider proportion of the population, to accord a more important role to lay believers, to give more appealing expression to the teachings and make them more readily accessible.

In earlier Buddhism the goal of religious striving had been to achieve the state of arhat or "worthy," one who has "nothing more to learn" and has escaped rebirth in the lower realms of existence. Even to reach this state, however, it was believed, required many lifetimes of strenuous exertion. But Mahayana urged men and women to aim for nothing less than the achievement of the highest level of enlightenment, that of Buddhahood. Enormous help in reaching this exalted goal, it was stressed, would come to them through figures known as bodhisattvas, beings who are dedicated not only to attaining enlightenment for themselves but, out of their immense compassion, to helping others to do likewise. Earlier Buddhism often described Shakyamuni Buddha as a bodhisattva in his previous existences, when he was still advancing toward enlightenment. But in Mahayana texts such as the Lotus Sutra the bodhisattvas are pictured as unlimited in number, all-seeing and all-caring, capable of extending boundless aid and succor to those who call upon them in sincere faith. Indeed, this great emphasis upon the role of the bodhisattva is one of the main characteristics that distinguish Mahayana thought from that of earlier Buddhism.

At first the proponents of these new Mahayana beliefs seem in many cases to have lived side by side in the same monasteries as the adherents of the earlier teachings, their religious practice centering around the worship of the Buddha's relics housed in the stupas or memorial towers. But doctrinal clashes arose from time to time and the two groups eventually drew apart. The Mahayana doctrines appear to have dominated in northwestern India, where they spread into the lands of Central Asia and thence into China. As a result, Chinese Buddhism was from the first overwhelmingly Mahayana in character, and it was this Mahayana version of the faith that in time was introduced to Korea, Japan, and Vietnam, where it continues in existence today.

THE WORLD OF THE LOTUS SUTRA

The Lotus Sutra depicts events that take place in a cosmic world of vast dimensions, a world in many ways reflecting traditional Indian views of the structure of the universe. For those who are not familiar with such views, it may be well to describe them here in brief. The world in which we live at present, it was believed, is made up of four continents ranged around a great central mountain, Mount Sumeru. We live in the continent located to the south, known as Jambudvipa or the "continent of the *jambu* trees." Outside of our present world there exist countless others spread out in all directions, some similarly made up of four continents, others realms presided over by various Buddhas. All these worlds, like our own, are caught up in a never-ending cycle of formation, continuance, decline, and disintegration, a process that takes place over vast kalpas or eons of time.

The ordinary beings living in our present world fall into six categories or occupy six realms of existence, arranged in hierarchical order in terms of their desirability. Lowest are the hell dwellers, beings who because of their evil actions in the past are compelled, for a time at least, to suffer in the various hells that exist beneath the earth, the most terrible of which is the Avichi hell or the hell of incessant suffering. On a slightly higher level are the hungry ghosts or spirits, beings who are tormented by endless hunger and craving. Above this is the level of beasts or beings of animal nature, and above that the realm of the *asuras*, demons who are pictured in Indian mythology as constantly engaged in angry warfare. These first three or four realms represent the "evil paths," the lowest, most painful and undesirable states of existence.

Above these is the fifth level, the realm of human beings, and the sixth, that of the heavenly beings or gods. The gods, though they lead far happier lives than the beings in the other realms, are doomed in time to die. Whatever the realm, all the beings in these six realms repeat the never-ending cycle of death and rebirth, moving up or down from one level to another depending upon the good or evil deeds they have committed, but never gaining release from the cycle.

To these six lower worlds or levels Mahayana Buddhism adds four more, the "holy states," representative of the life of enlightenment. On the seventh level are the *shravakas* or voice-hearers. This term, by which they are known in the Lotus Sutra, originally referred to the Buddha's disciples, those who had entered the Buddhist Order and learned the doctrines and practices directly from him, though later it came to refer to those monks and nuns who followed the teachings of early Buddhism such as the four noble truths and strove to attain the state of arhat. Once they attained that state they ceased their endeavors, convinced that they had gained the highest goal possible for them.

Above these, on the eighth level, are the *pratyekabuddhas* or "self-enlightened ones," beings who have won an understanding of the truth through their own efforts but who make no effort to teach others or assist them to enlightenment. On the ninth level are the bodhisattvas, already described above, who out of compassion postpone their entry into Buddhahood and remain in the *saha* world to alleviate the sufferings of others. On the tenth and highest level are the Buddhas or the state of Buddhahood. It is this level, according to Mahayana doctrine, that all living beings should seek to attain, and which, it insists, they can in time attain if they will not content themselves with lesser goals but have faith in the Buddha and his teachings as these are embodied in the sacred scriptures.

Before passing on to a discussion of the particular doctrines set forth in the Lotus Sutra, there is one more aspect of the Mahayana worldview that must be touched upon, difficult though it is to treat in the limited space that can be allotted here. This is the concept of

Emptiness or Void (*shunyata*) which is so central to the whole Mahayana system of belief.

The concept, often described in English as "nondualism," is extremely hard for the mind to grasp or visualize, since the mind engages
constantly in the making of distinctions and nondualism represents
the rejection or transcendence of all distinctions. The world perceived
through the senses, the phenomenal world as we know it, was described in early Buddhism as "empty" because it was taught that all
such phenomena arise from causes and conditions, are in a constant
state of flux, and are destined to change and pass away in time. They
are also held to be "empty" in the sense that they have no inherent or
permanent characteristics by which they can be described, changing as
they do from instant to instant. But in Mahayana thought it became
customary to emphasize not the negative but rather the positive aspects or import of the doctrine of Emptiness. If all phenomena are
characterized by the quality of Emptiness, then Emptiness must constitute the unchanging and abiding nature of existence, and therefore
the absolute or unchanging world must be synonymous with the
phenomenal one. Hence all mental and physical distinctions that we
perceive or conceive of with our minds must be part of a single
underlying unity. It is this concept of Emptiness or nonduality that
leads the Mahayana texts to assert that *samsara*, the ordinary world
of suffering and cyclical birth and death, is in the end identical with
the world of nirvana, and that earthly desires are enlightenment.

THE PRINCIPAL DOCTRINES OF
THE LOTUS SUTRA

The Kumarajiva translation of the Lotus Sutra as it exists at present is
made up of twenty-eight chapters. Nearly all the chapters consist of a
combination of prose and verse passages. Verse form was used to make
it easier for the followers of the religion to memorize the teachings
and retain them in mind, and the *gathas* or verse passages were
probably composed first. Later, as the sutra moved toward its final
form, prose passages were added that incorporated the verse sections
into a continuous narrative. In the present arrangement of the text,
the verse sections usually repeat what has already been stated in a
preceding prose passage.

Like nearly all sutras, the Lotus begins with the Buddha's close disciple Ananda speaking the words, "This is what I heard." Ananda, who was present at all the Buddha's expositions of the Dharma or doctrine, then proceeds to describe the occasion when, at Mount Gridhrakuta or Eagle Peak near the city of Rajagriha, the Buddha preached the Lotus Sutra.

In these opening sentences we are still in the world of historical reality or possibility, in a setting in the outskirts of the city of Rajagriha in northern India in which Gautama or Shakyamuni very probably did in fact propound his doctrines in the sixth or fifth century BCE.

But as Ananda proceeds to describe the staggering number and variety of human, nonhuman, and heavenly beings who have gathered to listen to the Buddha's discourse, we realize that we have left the world of factual reality far behind. This is the first point to keep in mind in reading the Lotus Sutra. Its setting, its vast assembly of listeners, its dramatic occurrences in the end belong to a realm that totally transcends our ordinary concepts of time, space, and possibility. Again and again we are told of events that took place countless, indescribable numbers of kalpas or eons in the past, or of beings or worlds that are as numerous as the sands of millions and billions of Ganges rivers. Such "numbers" are in fact no more than pseudo-numbers or non-numbers, intended to impress on us the impossibility of measuring the immeasurable. They are not meant to convey any statistical data but simply to boggle the mind and jar it loose from its conventional concepts of time and space. For in the realm of Emptiness, time and space as we conceive them are meaningless; anywhere is the same as everywhere, and now, then, never, forever are all one.

After several astounding events that impress upon us the truly cosmic scale of the drama that is unfolding, the Buddha begins to preach. The first important point he wishes to convey is that there is only one vehicle or one path to salvation, that which leads to the goal of Buddhahood. Earlier in his preaching career, he had described three paths for the believer, what he calls the three vehicles. One was that of the *shravaka* or voice-hearer, which leads to the realm of the arhat. Second was that of the *pratyekabuddha,* the being who gains enlightenment by himself and for himself alone, and the third was that of the bodhisattva. But now, the Buddha tells us, these lesser paths or goals are to be set aside and all beings are to aim for the single goal of Buddhahood, the one and only vehicle to true enlightenment or perfect understanding, a state designated in the Lotus Sutra by the rather daunting Sanskrit term *anuttara-samyak-sambodhi*.

When asked why, if there is only the single vehicle or truth, the Buddha has earlier taught his followers the doctrine of the three vehicles, he replies that at that time they were not yet ready to comprehend or accept the highest truth. Therefore he had to employ what he terms an expedient means in order to lead them gradually along the road to greater understanding. He then illustrates his point through the famous parable of the burning house.

The first lesson the sutra wishes to teach, then, is that its doctrines, delivered by the Buddha some forty or more years after the start of his preaching career, which is how the Lotus Sutra depicts them, represent the highest level of truth, the summation of the Buddha's message, superseding his earlier pronouncements, which had only pro- visional validity.

In some Mahayana texts Shariputra and the other close disciples of the Buddha, who represent the Lesser Vehicle outlook and path of endeavor, are held up to ridicule or portrayed as figures of fun. But the prevailing mood of the Lotus Sutra is one of compassion, and in it the voice-hearers are shown responding to the Buddha's words with understanding and gratitude. In return, the Buddha bestows on each of them a prophecy of the attainment of Buddhahood in a future existence, and in many cases reveals the type of Buddha land each will preside over.

The mood of revelation and rejoicing continues in the chapters that follow as the Buddha names more persons who are assured of attaining Buddhahood. The company of nuns who are attending the assembly, headed by the Buddha's aunt, Mahaprajapati, and his wife in his younger years, Yashodhara, at one point grow apprehensive because their names have not been mentioned, but the Buddha assures them that they too are included in his predictions of Buddhahood.

All these monks and nuns have been personal followers of Shakya- muni Buddha, diligent in religious practice and faultless in their obser- vance of the rules of conduct, and it is hardly surprising to learn that their efforts are to be crowned with success. Truly surprising, however, is the prophecy set forth in chapter twelve concerning Devadatta, who gives his name to the chapter.

Devadatta is described in accounts of the life of Shakyamuni Buddha as a disciple and cousin of the Buddha who, though full of zeal at first, later grew envious of Shakyamuni, made several attempts on his life, and schemed to foment division in the Order. For these crimes, among the most heinous in the eyes of Buddhism, he was said to have fallen into hell alive. Yet in chapter twelve of the Lotus Sutra the Buddha reveals that in a past existence this epitome of evil was in fact a good friend and teacher of the Buddha, preaching the way of enlightenment for him, and that in an era to come, Devadatta will without fail become a Buddha himself. From this we learn that even the most depraved of persons can hope for salvation, and that in the realm of nondualism good and evil are not the eternal and mutually exclusive opposites we had supposed them to be.

Chapter twelve relates another affair of equally astounding import. In it, the bodhisattva Manjushri describes how he has been preaching the Lotus Sutra at the palace of the dragon king at the bottom of the sea. The *nagas* or dragons, it should be noted, are one of eight kinds of nonhuman beings who are believed to protect Buddhism. They were revered in early Indian folk religion and were taken over by Buddhism, whose scriptures often portray them as paying homage to the Buddha and seeking knowledge of his teachings.

Asked if there were any among his listeners who succeeded in gaining enlightenment, Manjushri mentions the daughter of the dragon king Sagara, a girl just turned eight, who was able to master all the teachings. The questioner expresses understandable skepticism, pointing out that even Shakyamuni himself required many eons of religious practice before he could achieve enlightenment.

The girl herself then appears and before the astonished assembly performs various acts that demonstrate she has in fact achieved the highest level of understanding and can "in an instant" attain Buddha-hood. Earlier Buddhism had asserted that women are gravely hampered in their religious endeavors by "five obstacles," one of which is the fact that they can never hope to attain Buddhahood. But all such assertions are here in the Lotus Sutra unequivocally thrust aside. The child is a dragon, a nonhuman being, she is of the female sex, and she has barely turned eight, yet she reaches the highest goal in the space of a moment. Once again the Lotus Sutra reveals that its revolutionary doctrines operate in a realm transcending all petty distinctions of sex or species, instant or eon.

These joyous revelations concerning the universal accessibility of Buddhahood, which occupy the middle chapters of the sutra, constitute the second important message of the work. The third is set forth in chapter sixteen. In chapter fifteen we are told how a vast multitude of bodhisattvas spring up from the earth in a miraculous manner in order that they may undertake the task of transmitting and protecting the teachings of the Buddha. When the Buddha is asked who these bodhisattvas are, he replies that they are persons whom he has taught and guided to enlightenment. His questioner quite naturally asks how Shakyamuni could possibly have taught and converted such immeasurable multitudes in the course of only forty years of preaching.

In chapter sixteen Shakyamuni reveals the answer to this riddle. The Buddha, he says, is an eternal being, ever present in the world, ever concerned for the salvation of all beings. He attained Buddhahood an incalculably distant time in the past, and has never ceased to abide in the world since then. He seems at times to pass away into nirvana, and at other times to make a new appearance in the world. But he does this only so that living beings will not take his presence for granted and be slack in their quest for enlightenment. His seeming disappearance is no more than an expedient means which he employs to encourage them in their efforts, one of many such expedients that he adopts in order to fit his teachings to the different natures and capacities of individual beings and insure that they will have relevance for all. From this we see that in the Lotus Sutra the Buddha, who had earlier been viewed as a historical personality, is now conceived as a being who transcends all boundaries of time and space, an ever-abiding principle of truth and compassion that exists everywhere and within all beings.

These then are the principal teachings of the Lotus Sutra, concepts that are basic to all Mahayana thought. In the sutra they are often very beautifully and persuasively expounded, especially in the various parables for which the Lotus is famous. But one should not approach the Lotus expecting to find in it a methodical exposition of a system of philosophy. Some of the most important principles of Buddhism are only touched upon in passing, as though the reader or hearer is expected to be acquainted with them already, while many of the more revolutionary doctrines are not presented in any orderly fashion or supported by careful or detailed arguments but rather thrust upon him with the suddenness of divine revelation.

The text, with its long lists of personages, its astronomical numbers, its formulaic language and frequent repetitions, its vivid parables, is incantatory in effect, appealing not so much to the intellect as to the emotions. It may be noted that in the early centuries of Buddhism it was customary not to put the teachings into written form but to transmit them orally, the works being committed to memory as had been the practice in earlier Indian religion. This was thought to be the proper way, the respectful way to transmit them and insure that they were not revealed to persons who were unqualified or unworthy to receive them. The formulaic language, the recapitulations in verse, the repetitions were all designed to assist the memory of the reciter, and these stylistic features were retained even after the scriptures had been put into written form.

Very early in the sutra the Buddha warns us that the wisdom of the Buddhas is extremely profound and difficult to comprehend, and this warning is repeated frequently in later chapters. The Lotus Sutra tells us at times that the Lotus Sutra is about to be preached, at other times it says that the Lotus Sutra has already been preached with such-and-such results, and at still other times it gives instructions on just how the Lotus Sutra is to be preached or enumerates in detail the merits that accrue to one who pays due honor to the text. But the reader may be forgiven if he comes away from the work wondering just which of the chapters that make it up was meant to be the Lotus Sutra itself. One writer has in fact been led to describe the sutra as a text "about a discourse that is never delivered, . . . a lengthy preface without a book."[1] This is no doubt because Mahayana Buddhism has always insisted that its highest truth can never in the end be expressed in words, since words immediately create the kind of distinctions that violate the unity of Emptiness. All the sutra can do, therefore, is to talk around it, leaving a hole in the middle where truth can reside.

1. George J. Tanabe, Jr. and Wilma Jane Tanabe, eds., *The Lotus Sutra in Japanese Culture* (Honolulu: University of Hawaii Press, 1989), p. 2 in the introductory chapter by Professor George Tanabe.

But of course in the view of religion there are other approaches to truth than merely through words and intellectual discourse. The sutra therefore exhorts the individual to approach the wisdom of the Buddhas through the avenue of faith and religious practice. The profound influence which the Lotus Sutra has exerted upon the cultural and religious life of the countries of eastern Asia is due as much to its function as a guide to devotional practice as to the actual ideas that it expounds. It calls upon us to act out the sutra with our bodies and minds rather than merely reading it, and in that way to enter into its meaning.

Much of the Lotus Sutra is taken up with injunctions to the believer to "accept and uphold, read, recite, copy and teach" it to others, and with descriptions of the bountiful merits to be gained by such action, as well as warnings of the evil effects of speaking ill of the sutra and its practices. In addition, one is encouraged to make offerings to the Buddhas and bodhisattvas, to the stupas or memorial towers, and to the monastic Order. Flowers, incense, music, and chants of praise are the customary offerings cited in the sutra, along with food, clothing, bedding, and other daily necessities in the case of members of the Order. Gold, silver, gems and other valuables are also listed among the offerings, but lest this would seem to put the rich at an advantage, the sutra early on emphasizes that it is the spirit in which the offering is made rather than the article itself that is important. Even a tower of sand fashioned by children in play, if offered in the proper spirit, will be acceptable in the sight of the Buddha and bring reward, we are told. It may be noted that the animal sacrifices so central to the earlier Vedic religion were rejected by Buddhism as abhorrent. One chapter of the Lotus does in fact describe a bodhisattva who burned his own body as a form of sacrifice, but the passage is clearly meant to be taken metaphorically. Despite this fact, some believers of later times, in their eagerness to emulate the bodhisattva's example, have interpreted it with tragic literalness.

Most famous and influential of the devotional chapters of the Lotus Sutra are those with which the work closes and which portray various bodhisattvas who can render particular aid and protection to the believer. Noteworthy among these is chapter twenty-five, which centers on a bodhisattva named Avalokiteshvara or Perceiver of the World's Sounds, known in China as Kuan-yin and in Japan as Kannon. The chapter relates in very concrete terms the wonderful types of assistance that the bodhisattva can render to persons of all different social levels and walks of life, ranging from kings and high ministers to traveling merchants or criminals in chains. In order to make his teaching and aid most readily acceptable to all kinds of beings, the bodhisattva is prepared to take on thirty-three different forms, matching his form to that of the being who calls upon him, whether that being be man or woman, exalted or humble, human or nonhuman in nature. Through chapters such as these, which have been recited with fervor by countless devotees over the centuries, the sutra has brought comfort and hope to all levels of society.

Because of its importance as an expression of basic Mahayana thought, its appeal as a devotional work, its dramatic scenes and memorable parables, the Lotus, as already emphasized, has exerted an incalculable influence upon the culture of East Asia. More commentaries have been written on it than on any other Buddhist scripture. The great works of Chinese and Japanese literature such as *The Dream of the Red Chamber* and *The Tale of Genji* are deeply imbued with its ideas and imagery, and its scenes are among the most frequently depicted in the religious art of the area.

The Lotus is not so much an integral work as a collection of religious texts, an anthology of sermons, stories and devotional manuals, some speaking with particular force to persons of one type or in one set of circumstances, some to those of another type or in other circumstances. This is no doubt one reason why it has had such broad and lasting appeal over the ages and has permeated so deeply into the cultures that have been exposed to it.

The present translation is offered in the hope that through it readers of English may come to appreciate something of the power and appeal of the Lotus Sutra, and that among its wealth of profound religious ideas and striking imagery they may find passages that speak compellingly to them as well.

BURTON WATSON

TRANSLATOR'S NOTE

Why another English translation of the Lotus Sutra, one may ask, when there are several already in existence? First, I would reply, because language changes and translations grow old. The great works of world literature deserve to be translated again and again so that they will continue to be in language that is appealing to contemporary readers. The earliest English translation of the Lotus Sutra, that done by Kern from a Sanskrit version and published in 1884, assuredly no longer is.

Second, because each translator has a certain kind of reader in mind as the work progresses, and certain aspects of the text he or she is especially concerned to do justice to in the translation, perhaps at the expense of other important aspects of the original. The present translation, as should be apparent from the translator's introduction, is designed for readers who have no special background in Buddhist studies or Asian literature. Thus, for example, Sanskrit names and terms have been romanized in a form that differs slightly from the standard form used in works intended for specialists, a form that it is hoped will help guide them to the correct pronunciation; standard romanization for all such words may be found in the Glossary at the back of the book. The Glossary will also provide background information on personal and place names and technical terms that recur frequently in the text.

The translation, it is hoped, will not only convey the ideas for which the work is so important, but at the same time give some sense of its rich literary appeal. The translation is intended to be in straightforward modern English. No attempt has been made, as in some translations of Buddhist scriptures, to impart a "religious" tone by employing an archaic or biblical-sounding style. Despite the often-noted resemblance between one of its parables and the New Testament story of the prodigal son, the Lotus Sutra, particularly in its thought, is rather far removed from the world of the Bible.

Why, one may also ask, if the Lotus Sutra is a work of Indian Buddhism, has the translation been made from the Kumarajiva Chinese translation of the text rather than from one of the Sanskrit versions? First, as already mentioned in my introduction, though we do not know what language the Lotus Sutra was first composed in, it was very probably not Sanskrit, and therefore the Sanskrit versions of the text are already one step removed from the original. Second, none of the extant Sanskrit versions are as early in date as Kumarajiva's Chinese translation, done in 406, and all differ in some respects from his version. Thus his almost certainly represents an earlier version of the text, one nearer to the original. But most important of all, Kumarajiva's Chinese translation is the version in which the Lotus Sutra has been known and read over the centuries throughout the countries of eastern Asia. Buddhism died out in India long ago and the Sanskrit versions of the text were lost for many hundreds of years, only coming to light again in recent times. Today no one but a handful of scholars read the Lotus Sutra in its Sanskrit versions, whereas Kumarajiva's text is read and recited daily by millions of priests and lay believers of East Asia. It is the language and imagery of the Chinese Lotus Sutra that has molded the religious life and thought of the peoples of that part of the world and made its way into their art and literature. So it seemed wholly justifiable to make the English translation from this still living and vital version of the scripture.

For readers not familiar with the remarkable story of Kumarajiva's life, it may be mentioned here that he lived from 344 to 413 and was a native of the small state of Kucha in Central Asia. His father was an Indian of distinguished family who later in life became a Buddhist monk. His mother was a younger sister of the ruler of Kucha. He entered the Buddhist Order as a boy, and with his mother, who had become a nun, traveled extensively around India, acquiring a profound knowledge of Buddhist texts and teachings. Returning to Kucha, he devoted himself there to the propagation of Mahayana Buddhism.

In time his fame as a Buddhist scholar reached China. The Chinese ruler, eager to have so distinguished a religious figure at his own court, dispatched one of his generals to invade Kucha and bring Kumarajiva to the Chinese capital at Ch'ang-an. Because of a change in the ruling dynasty, Kumarajiva was detained for a number of years in Liang-chou in Kansu, but finally reached Ch'ang-an in 401. There, with the support of the ruler, he immediately embarked on a strenuous translation program, producing in rapid succession a series of authoritative Chinese versions of important Buddhist sutras and treatises, thirty-five works in all, among them the Lotus Sutra. He was greatly aided in his work by a large body of Chinese disciples and scholar-monks who carefully checked his translations against earlier versions, discussed the meaning with him, and helped him to polish the wording of his own versions. This is no doubt one reason why Kumarajiva's translation of the Lotus Sutra is so superior to other Chinese translations and why it has been so widely and enthusiastically read.

The origin of the present translation goes back to a day in Tokyo in December 1973 when I had an opportunity to meet and talk with President Daisaku Ikeda, head of the Soka Gakkai International and a world leader in the Buddhist movement. When President Ikeda learned that most of my translation work was from texts in classical Chinese, he said, "In that case, you must do us a new translation of the Kumarajiva Lotus Sutra!" The project appealed to me immediately, and though it was some years before I could begin actual work, I am extremely grateful for the opportunity it has afforded me to deal with a text of such lasting importance.

The translation was prepared with the assistance of the Nichiren

Shoshu International Center in Tokyo, which is connected with Soka Gakkai International. The translation is based on the Chinese text and Japanese *yomikudashi* found in the *Myōhō-renge-kyō narabi ni kaiketsu*, compiled and edited by the Soka Gakkai and published in Tokyo in 1961. The Chinese text of the Kumarajiva translation was fixed long ago and there are no significant textual variations. I would like here to express my deep gratitude to the many persons associated with Soka Gakkai International and the Nichiren Shoshu International Center who lent their assistance to the undertaking. They not only checked over my translation with care and thoroughness, but offered invaluable advice at many points on questions of interpretation and presentation.

A word may be said here as to the sort of problems in interpretation that arose. Classical Chinese, the language of the Kumarajiva Lotus, is highly spare and compressed in style, and hence often ambiguous in meaning or construction and open to varying interpretations. Thus, for example, it is easy to tell where a passage of direct speech begins, but often difficult to determine exactly where it ends. Verbs frequently lack an expressed subject, and a quite legitimate case can be made for several different interpretations of the passage. One must often guess at the tense of a verb, or whether a noun is to be taken as singular or plural. Particularly in the verse sections, where the language has been unusually compressed or distorted in order to fit into lines of uniform length, the meaning can sometimes scarcely be made out at all without consulting the parallel passage in the prose section.

Because of such recurring problems and ambiguities, no two translators of the Chinese will ever come up with exactly identical renderings of the text. This does not mean in most cases that one translator is wrong and the other right, but simply that they have made different choices in their interpretation. In the present translation I have tried to render the text in the way that it has traditionally been understood in China and Japan. That is why I have carefully taken into consideration the Japanese *yomikudashi* reading in the edition cited above, which rearranges the Chinese characters of the text so that they conform to the patterns of Japanese syntax. This reading is based on the interpretation of the text followed by Nichiren (1222–1282), the founder of Nichiren Buddhism in Japan, who throughout his life constantly lectured on the Lotus Sutra to his disciples and lay followers and gave detailed expositions of its teachings. His interpretation is in turn based on the commentaries on the Lotus Sutra by the great scholar of Chinese Buddhism, Chih-i (538–597), the founder of the T'ien-t'ai school.

It may be noted here that Chih-i in his commentaries on the Lotus Sutra developed an extremely complex and sophisticated hermeneutical system by which he attempted to bring out the sutra's deepest meaning and define its position and importance in the body of the Buddhist writings as a whole. This system was further elaborated and refined in subcommentaries on Chih-i's works written by his disciples or later scholars of the T'ien-t'ai school. To fully appreciate the way in which the Lotus Sutra has traditionally been interpreted in East Asian Buddhist circles, one would ideally have to master the ideas and terminology of this system of exegesis. But simply to describe the system adequately would require almost as much space as has been devoted to the translation itself, and would no doubt deter readers from responding to the translation in a direct and personal manner. In the translator's introduction and glossary I have therefore made little reference to this system, but have tried to concentrate on doctrines and motifs that are explicit in the Lotus itself.

But to return to the translation, the single most troublesome problem faced in the translation was how best to handle the Chinese word *fa*, which is used in Buddhist Chinese to render the Sanskrit word *dharma*. Sometimes in the Chinese Lotus the word *fa* seems to refer to the Truth as taught in Buddhism or the doctrine as a whole, in which cases it has been translated "Dharma" or "the Law." But sometimes it is preceded by the pluralizing word *chu*; to translate it in such cases as "the Laws" would give, it was felt, too legalistic a tone, and it has therefore been rendered as "doctrines" or "teachings." The word *dharma* in Sanskrit can also mean a "thing" or a phenomenon, one of the elements that make up existence, and there are places in the Lotus where this meaning is clearly intended. Indeed, one of the most famous phrases in the Chinese version of the sutra is *chu-fa shih-hsiang* (in Japanese *shohō jissō*), which occurs in chapter two and which in the present translation has been rendered as "the true aspect of all phenomena." In still other cases *fa* seems to mean merely a rule, a method, or an approach, and has accordingly been rendered by some such equivalent.

One hates to impose distinctions on the translation where they do not exist in the original. But to translate *fa* as "dharma" in all these different cases would not only make for awkward English in places but would fail to convey the real meaning of the passage. I therefore decided to translate the word differently in different contexts. I may not always have made the best choice in deciding what English equivalent to use, but the reader may be assured that I gave careful thought to all such places.

OTHER COMPLETE ENGLISH TRANSLATIONS OF THE LOTUS SUTRA

The Saddharmapundarika; or, The Lotus of the True Law. Tr. by Jan Hendrik Kern. Sacred Books of the East, vol. 21. Oxford: Clarendon Press, 1884.

The first English translation, done from a Sanskrit version of the text that, according to Kern, is dated 1039.

The Sutra of the Lotus Flower of the Wonderful Law. Tr. by Senchu Murano. Tokyo: Nichiren Shu Headquarters, 1974.

Translation of the Kumarajiva version of the Lotus Sutra. Brief introduction, very extensive glossaries, particularly useful to readers with a knowledge of the Japanese readings of Buddhist names and terms.

The Threefold Lotus Sutra: The Sutra of Innumerable Meanings; The Sutra of the Lotus Flower of the Wonderful Law; The Sutra of Meditation on the Bodhisattva Universal Virtue. Tr. by Bunnō Katō, Yoshirō Tamura, and Kojiro Miyasaka. Tokyo: Kosei, 1975.

Translation of the Kumarajiva version of the Lotus, plus two other short sutras that, from the time of Chih-i, have been regarded as an introduction and postscript respectively to the Lotus. Brief introduction and extensive glossary.

Scripture of the Lotus Blossom of the Fine Dharma. Tr. by Leon Hurvitz. New York: Columbia University Press, 1976.

Translation of the Kumarajiva version of the Lotus. Contains a preface, glossary, and extensive section of passages translated from a Sanskrit version of the text to show where and how the Sanskrit differs from the Chinese translation of Kumarajiva. An invaluable work of scholarship.

The Lotus Sutra: The White Lotus of the Marvelous Law. Tr. by Tsugunari Kubo and Akira Yuyama. Tokyo and Berkeley: Bukkyo Dendo Kyokai, 1991.

Translation of the Kumarajiva version of the Lotus. Brief translator's introduction, Sanskrit glossary, and selected bibliography.

THE
ESSENTIAL
LOTUS

2

EXPEDIENT MEANS

At that time the World-Honored One calmly arose from his samadhi and addressed Shariputra, saying: "The wisdom of the Buddhas is infinitely profound and immeasurable. The door to this wisdom is difficult to understand and difficult to enter. Not one of the voice-hearers or pratyekabuddhas is able to comprehend it.

"What is the reason for this? A Buddha has personally attended a hundred, a thousand, ten thousand, a million, a countless number of Buddhas and has fully carried out an immeasurable number of religious practices. He has exerted himself bravely and vigorously, and his name is universally known. He has realized the Law that is profound and never known before, and preaches it in accordance with what is appropriate, yet his intention is difficult to understand.

"Shariputra, ever since I attained Buddhahood I have through various causes and various similes widely expounded my teachings and have used countless expedient means to guide living beings and cause them to renounce their attachments. Why is this? Because the Thus Come One is fully possessed of both expedient means and the paramita of wisdom.

"Shariputra, the wisdom of the Thus Come One is expansive and profound. He has immeasurable [mercy], unlimited [eloquence], power, fearlessness, concentration, emancipation, and samadhis, and has deeply entered the boundless and awakened to the Law never before attained.

"Shariputra, the Thus Come One knows how to make various kinds of distinctions and to expound the teachings skillfully. His words are soft and gentle and can delight the hearts of the assembly.

"Shariputra, to sum it up: the Buddha has fully realized the Law that is limitless, boundless, never attained before.

"But stop, Shariputra, I will say no more. Why? Because what the Buddha has achieved is the rarest and most difficult-to-understand Law. The true aspect of all phenomena can only be understood and shared between Buddhas. This reality consists of the appearance, nature, entity, power, influence, inherent cause, relation, latent effect, manifest effect, and their consistency from beginning to end."

At that time the World-Honored One, wishing to state his meaning once more, spoke in verse form, saying:

> The hero of the world is unfathomable.
> Among heavenly beings or the people of the world,
> among all living beings,
> none can understand the Buddha.
> The Buddha's power, fearlessness,
> emancipation and samadhis
> and the Buddha's other attributes
> no one can reckon or fathom.
> Earlier, under the guidance of countless Buddhas
> he fully acquired and practiced various ways,
> profound, subtle and wonderful doctrines
> that are hard to see and hard to understand.

For immeasurable millions of kalpas
he has been practicing these ways
until in the place of practice he achieved the goal.
I have already come to see and know completely
this great goal and recompense,
the meaning of these various natures and characteristics.
I and the other Buddhas of the ten directions
can now understand these things.
This Law cannot be described,
words fall silent before it.
Among the other kinds of living beings
there are none who can comprehend it,
except the many bodhisattvas
who are firm in the power of faith.
The many disciples of the Buddhas
in the past have given offerings to the Buddhas,
have already cut off all outflows
and now are dwelling in their last incarnation.
But even such persons as they
have not the power needed.
Even if the whole world
were filled with men like Shariputra,
though they exhausted their thoughts and pooled
    their capacities,
they could not fathom the Buddha's knowledge.
Even if ten directions
were all filled with men like Shariputra
or like the other disciples,
though they filled the lands in the ten directions
and exhausted their thoughts and pooled their capacities,
still they could not understand it.
If pratyekabuddhas, acute in understanding,
without outflows, in their last incarnation,
should fill the worlds in the ten directions,
as numerous as bamboos in a grove,
though they should join together with one mind
for a million or for countless kalpas,
hoping to conceive of the Buddha's true wisdom,

they could not understand the smallest part of it.
If bodhisattvas newly embarked on their course
should give offerings to numberless Buddhas,
completely mastering the intent of the various doctrines
and also able to preach the Law effectively,
like so many rice and hemp plants, bamboos or reeds,
filling the lands in the ten directions,
with a single mind, with their wonderful knowledge,
for kalpas numerous as Ganges sands
should all together pool their thoughts and capacities,
they could not understand the Buddha's knowledge.
If bodhisattvas who never regress,
their number like Ganges sands,
with a single mind should join in pondering and seeking,
they could not understand it either.
I also announce to you, Shariputra,
that this profound, subtle and wonderful Law
without outflows, incomprehensible,
I have now attained in full.
Only I understand its characteristics,
and the Buddhas of the ten directions do likewise.
Shariputra, you should know
that the words of the various Buddhas never differ.
Toward the Law preached by the Buddhas
you must cultivate a great power of faith.
The World-Honored One has long expounded his doctrines
and now must reveal the truth.
I announce this to the assembly of voice-hearers
and to those who seek the vehicle of the pratyekabuddha:
I have enabled people to escape the bonds of suffering
and to attain nirvana.
The Buddha, through the power of expedient means,
has shown them the teachings of the three vehicles,
prying living beings loose from this or that attachment
and allowing them to attain release.

At that time among the great assembly there were voice-hearers,
arhats whose outflows had come to an end, Ajnata Kaundinya and the

others, twelve hundred persons. And there were monks, nuns, laymen and laywomen who had conceived a desire to become voice-hearers or pratyekabuddhas. Each of these had this thought: Now for what reason does the World-Honored One so earnestly praise expedient means and state that the Law attained by the Buddha is profound and difficult to understand, that it is very difficult to comprehend the meaning of the words he preaches, that not one of the voice-hearers or pratyekabuddhas can do so? If the Buddha preaches but one doctrine of emancipation, then we too should be able to attain this Law and reach the state of nirvana. We cannot follow the gist of what he is saying now.

At that time Shariputra understood the doubts that were in the minds of the four kinds of believers, and he himself had not fully comprehended. So he addressed the Buddha, saying, "World-Honored One, what causes and conditions lead you to earnestly praise expedient means, the foremost device of the Buddhas, the profound, subtle and wonderful Law that is difficult to understand? From times past I have never heard this kind of preaching from the Buddha. Now the four kinds of believers all have doubts. We beg that the World-Honored One will expound this matter. For what reason does the World-Honored One earnestly praise this Law that is profound, subtle and wonderful, difficult to understand?"

At that time Shariputra, wishing to state his meaning once more, spoke in verse form, saying:

> Sun of wisdom, great sage and venerable one,
> at long last you preach this Law.
> You yourself declare you have attained
> power, fearlessness, samadhis,
> concentration, emancipation, and these other attributes,
> and the Law that is beyond comprehension.
> This Law attained in the place of practice
> no one is capable of questioning you about.
> "My intention is hard to fathom,
> and no one can question me."
> No one questions, yet you yourself preach,
> praising the path you walk on.
> Your wisdom is very subtle and wonderful,
> that which all the Buddhas attain.

The arhats who are without outflows
and those who seek nirvana
now have all fallen into the net of doubt,
wondering for what reason the Buddha preaches this.
Those who seek to become pratyekabuddhas,
monks and nuns,
heavenly beings, dragons and spirits,
along with the gandharvas and others,
look at one another, filled with perplexity,
gazing upward at the most honored of two-legged beings.
What is the meaning of all this?
I beg the Buddha to explain it for us.
Among the assembly of voice-hearers
the Buddha has said I am foremost,
yet now I lack the wisdom
to solve these doubts and perplexities.
Have I in fact grasped the ultimate Law,
or am I still on the path of practice?
The sons born from the Buddha's mouth
press palms together, gaze upward and wait.
We beg you to put forth subtle and wonderful sounds
and at this time explain to us how it really is.
The heavenly beings, dragons, spirits, and the others,
their numbers like Ganges sands,
the bodhisattvas seeking to be Buddhas
in a great force of eighty thousand,
as well as the wheel-turning sage kings
come from ten thousands of millions of lands,
all press their palms and with reverent minds
wish to hear the teaching of perfect endowment.

At that time the Buddha addressed Shariputra, saying, "Stop, stop! There is no need to speak further. If I speak of this matter, then the heavenly and human beings throughout the worlds will all be astonished and doubtful."

Shariputra once more spoke to the Buddha, saying, "World-Honored One, we beg you to preach! We beg you to preach! What is the reason? Because this assembly of countless hundreds, thousands, ten thousands, millions of asamkhyas of living beings in the past have seen the Buddhas; their faculties are vigorous and acute and their wisdom is bright. If they hear the Buddha preach, they will be capable of reverent belief."

At that time Shariputra, wishing to state his meaning once more, spoke in verse form, saying:

> Dharma King, none more highly honored,
> speak, we beg you, without reserve!
> In this assembly of numberless beings
> are those capable of reverent belief.

The Buddha repeated, "Stop, Shariputra! If I speak of this matter, the heavenly and human beings and asuras throughout the worlds will all be astonished and doubtful. The monks who are overbearingly arrogant will fall into a great pit."

At that time the World-Honored One repeated what he had said in verse form:

> Stop, stop, no need to speak!
> My Law is wonderful and difficult to ponder.
> Those who are overbearingly arrogant
> when they hear it will never show reverent belief.

At that time Shariputra once more spoke to the Buddha, saying, "World-Honored One, we beg you to preach! We beg you to preach! In this assembly at present the persons like myself number in the hundreds, thousands, ten thousands, millions. In age after age we have already attended the Buddhas and received instruction. People of this kind are certain to be capable of reverent belief. Throughout the long night they will gain peace and rest and will enjoy many benefits."

At that time Shariputra, wishing to state his meaning once more, spoke in verse form, saying:

> Supremely honored among two-legged beings,
> we beg you to preach this foremost Law.
> I who am regarded as the Buddha's eldest son
> ask you to favor us by preaching distinctions.

The countless members of this assembly
are capable of according reverent belief to this Law.
The Buddhas have already in age after age
taught and converted them in this manner.
All with a single mind and palms pressed together
desire to hear and receive the Buddha's words.
I and the other twelve hundred of our group,
as well as the others who seek to become Buddhas,
beg that for the sake of this assembly
you will favor us by preaching distinctions.
When we hear this Law
we will be filled with great joy.

At that time the World-Honored One said to Shariputra, "Three times you have stated your earnest request. How can I do other than preach? Now you must listen attentively and carefully ponder. For your sake I will now analyze and explain the matter."

When he had spoken these words, there were some five thousand monks, nuns, laymen and laywomen in the assembly who immediately rose from their seats, bowed to the Buddha, and withdrew. What was the reason for this? These persons had roots of guilt that were deep and manifold, and in addition they were overbearingly arrogant. What they had not attained they supposed they had attained, what they had not understood they supposed they had understood. And because they had this failing, they did not remain where they were.

The World-Honored One was silent and did not try to detain them.

At this time the Buddha said to Shariputra, "Now this assembly of mine is free of branches and leaves, made up solely of the steadfast and truthful. Shariputra, it is well that these persons of overbearing arrogance have withdrawn. Now listen carefully and I will preach for you."

Shariputra said, "So be it, World-Honored One. We are eager to listen!"

The Buddha said to Shariputra, "A wonderful Law such as this is preached by the Buddhas, the Thus Come Ones, at certain times. But like the blooming of the udumbara, such times come very seldom. Shariputra, you and the others must believe me. The words that the Buddhas preach are not empty or false.

"Shariputra, the Buddhas preach the Law in accordance with what is appropriate, but the meaning is difficult to understand. Why is this? Because we employ countless expedient means, discussing causes and conditions and using words of simile and parable to expound the teachings. This Law is not something that can be understood through pondering or analysis. Only those who are Buddhas can understand it. Why is this? Because the Buddhas, the World-Honored Ones, appear in the world for one great reason alone. Shariputra, what does it mean to say that the Buddhas, the World-Honored Ones, appear in the world for one great reason alone?

"The Buddhas, the World-Honored Ones, wish to open the door of Buddha wisdom to all living beings, to allow them to attain purity. That is why they appear in the world. They wish to show the Buddha wisdom to living beings, and therefore they appear in the world. They wish to cause living beings to awaken to the Buddha wisdom, and therefore they appear in the world. They wish to induce living beings to enter the path of Buddha wisdom, and therefore they appear in the world. Shariputra, this is the one great reason for which the Buddhas appear in the world."

The Buddha said to Shariputra, "The Buddhas, the Thus Come Ones, simply teach and convert the bodhisattvas. All the things they do are at all times done for this one purpose. They simply wish to show the Buddha wisdom to living beings and enlighten them to it.

"Shariputra, the Thus Come Ones have only a single Buddha vehicle which they employ in order to preach the Law to living beings. They do not have any other vehicle, a second one or a third one.[1] Shariputra, the Law preached by all the Buddhas of the ten directions is the same as this.

"Shariputra, the Buddhas of the past used countless numbers of expedient means, various causes and conditions, and words of simile and parable in order to expound the doctrines for the sake of living beings. These doctrines are all for the sake of the one Buddha vehicle. These living beings, by listening to the doctrines of the Buddhas, are all eventually able to attain wisdom embracing all species.

"Shariputra, when the Buddhas of the future make their appearance

1. Or perhaps the meaning is "They do not have any other vehicle, not two vehicles or three." The Chinese permits either reading, and Chinese Buddhist sects have disagreed as to which interpretation to follow.

in the world, they too will use countless numbers of expedient means, various causes and conditions, and words of simile and parable in order to expound the doctrines for the sake of living beings. These doctrines will all be for the sake of the one Buddha vehicle. And these living beings, by listening to the doctrines of the Buddhas, will all eventually be able to attain wisdom embracing all species.

"Shariputra, the Buddhas, the World-Honored Ones, who exist at present in the countless hundreds, thousands, ten thousands, and millions of Buddha lands in the ten directions, benefit and bring peace and happiness to living beings in large measure. These Buddhas too use countless numbers of expedient means, various causes and conditions, and words of simile and parable in order to expound the doctrines for the sake of living beings. These doctrines are all for the sake of the one Buddha vehicle. And these living beings, by listening to the doctrines of the Buddhas, are all eventually able to attain wisdom embracing all species.

"Shariputra, these Buddhas simply teach and convert the bodhisattvas. They do it because they wish to show the Buddha wisdom to living beings. They do it because they wish to use the Buddha wisdom to enlighten living beings. They do it because they wish to cause living beings to enter the path of Buddha wisdom.

"Shariputra, I too will now do the same. I know that living beings have various desires, attachments that are deeply implanted in their minds. Taking cognizance of this basic nature of theirs, I will therefore use various causes and conditions, words of simile and parable, and the power of expedient means and expound the Law for them. Shariputra, I do this so that all of them may attain the one Buddha vehicle and wisdom embracing all species.

"Shariputra, in the worlds of the ten directions, there are not two vehicles, much less three! Shariputra, the Buddhas appear in evil worlds of five impurities. These are the so-called impurity of the age, impurity of desire, impurity of living beings, impurity of view, and impurity of life span.

"Shariputra, when the age is impure and the times are chaotic, then the defilements of living beings are grave, they are greedy and jealous and put down roots that are not good. Because of this, the Buddhas, utilizing the power of expedient means, apply distinctions to the one Buddha vehicle and preach as though it were three.

"Shariputra, if any of my disciples should claim to be an arhat or a pratyekabuddha and yet does not heed or understand that the Buddhas, the Thus Come Ones, simply teach and convert the bodhisattvas, then he is no disciple of mine, he is no arhat or pratyekabuddha.

"Again, Shariputra, if there should be monks or nuns who claim that they have already attained the status of arhat, that this is their last incarnation, that they have reached the final nirvana, and that therefore they have no further intention of seeking anuttara-samyak-sambodhi, then you should understand that such as these are all persons of overbearing arrogance. Why do I say this? Because if there are monks who have truly attained the status of arhat, then it would be unthinkable that they should fail to believe this Law. The only exception would be in a time after the Buddha had passed away, when there was no Buddha present in the world. Why is this? Because after the Buddha has passed away it will be difficult to find anyone who can embrace, recite, and understand the meaning of sutras such as this. But if persons at that time encounter another Buddha, then they will attain decisive understanding with regard to this Law.

"Shariputra, you and the others should with a single mind believe and accept the words of the Buddha. The words of the Buddhas, the Thus Come Ones, are not empty or false. There is no other vehicle, there is only the one Buddha vehicle."

At that time the World-Honored One, wishing to state his meaning once more, spoke in verse form, saying:

> There are monks and nuns
> who behave with overbearing arrogance,
> laymen full of self-esteem,
> laywomen who are lacking in faith.
> Among the four kinds of believers, the likes of these
> number five thousand.
> They fail to see their own errors,
> are heedless and remiss with regard to the precepts,
> clinging to their shortcomings, unwilling to change.
> But these persons of small wisdom have already left;
> the chaff among this assembly
> has departed in the face of the Buddha's authority.
> These persons were of paltry merit and virtue,

incapable of receiving this Law.
This assembly is now free of branches and leaves,
made up only of those steadfast and truthful.
Shariputra, listen carefully,
for the Law which the Buddhas have attained,
through the power of countless expedient means
they preach for the benefit of living beings.
The thoughts that are in the minds of living beings,
the different types of paths they follow,
their various desires and natures,
the good and bad deeds they have done in previous existences—
all these the Buddha takes cognizance of,
and then he employs causes, similes and parables,
words that embody the power of expedient means,
in order to gladden and please them all.
Sometimes he preaches sutras,
verses, stories of the previous lives of disciples,
stories of the previous lives of the Buddha, of
    unheard-of things.
At other times he preaches regarding causes and conditions,
uses similes, parables, passages of poetry
or discourses.
For those of dull capacities who delight in a little Law,
who greedily cling to birth and death,
who, despite the innumerable Buddhas,
fail to practice the profound and wonderful way
but are perplexed and confused by a host of troubles—
for these I preach nirvana.
I devise these expedient means
and so cause them to enter into the Buddha wisdom.
Up to now I have never told you
that you were certain to attain the Buddha way.
The reason I never preached in that manner
was that the time to preach so had not yet come.
But now is the very time
when I must decisively preach the Great Vehicle.
I use these nine devices,
adapting them to the living beings when I preach,

my basic aim being to lead them into the Great Vehicle,
and that is why I preach this sutra.
There are sons of the Buddha whose minds are pure,
who are gentle and of acute capacities,
who under innumerable Buddhas
have practiced the profound and wonderful way.
For these sons of the Buddha
I preach this sutra of the Great Vehicle.
And I predict that these persons
in a future existence will attain the Buddha way.
Because deep in their minds they think of the Buddha
and practice and uphold the pure precepts,
they are assured they will attain Buddhahood,
and hearing this, their whole bodies are filled with great joy.
The Buddha knows their minds and their practices
and therefore preaches for them the Great Vehicle.
When the voice-hearers and bodhisattvas
hear this Law that I preach,
as soon as they have heard one verse
they will all without doubt be certain of attaining Buddhahood.
In the Buddha lands of the ten directions
there is only the Law of the one vehicle,
there are not two, there are not three,
except when the Buddha preaches so as an expedient means,
merely employing provisional names and terms
in order to conduct and guide living beings
and preach to them the Buddha wisdom.
The Buddhas appear in the world
solely for this one reason, which is true;
the other two are not the truth.
Never do they use a lesser vehicle
to save living beings and ferry them across.
The Buddha himself dwells in this Great Vehicle,
and adorned with the power of meditation and wisdom
that go with the Law he has attained,
he uses it to save living beings.
He himself testifies to the unsurpassed way,
the Great Vehicle, the Law in which all things are equal.

If I used a lesser vehicle
to convert even one person,
I would be guilty of stinginess and greed,
but such a thing would be impossible.
If a person will believe and take refuge in the Buddha,
the Thus Come One will never deceive him,
nor will he ever show greed or jealousy,
for he has rooted out evil from among the phenomena.
Therefore throughout the ten directions
the Buddha alone is without fear.
I adorn my body with the special characteristics
and shine my light upon the world.
I am honored by numberless multitudes
and for them I preach the emblem of the reality of things.
Shariputra, you should know
that at the start I took a vow,
hoping to make all persons
equal to me, without any distinction between us,
and what I long ago hoped for
has now been fulfilled.
I have converted all living beings
and caused them all to enter the Buddha way.
If when I encounter living beings
I were in all cases to teach them the Buddha way,
those without wisdom would become confused
and in their bewilderment would fail to accept my teachings.
I know that such living beings
have never in the past cultivated good roots
but have stubbornly clung to the five desires,
and their folly and craving have given rise to affliction.
Their desires are the cause
whereby they fall into the three evil paths,
revolving wheel-like through the six realms of existence
and undergoing every sort of suffering and pain.
Having received a tiny form in the womb,
in existence after existence they constantly grow to maturity.
Persons of meager virtue and small merit,
they are troubled and beset by manifold sufferings.

They stray into the dense forest of mistaken views,
debating as to what exists and what does not,
and in the end cling to such views,
embracing all sixty-two of them.[2]
They are profoundly committed to false and empty doctrines,
holding firmly to them, unable to set them aside.
Arrogant and puffed up with self-importance,
fawning and devious, insincere in mind,
for a thousand, ten thousand, a million kalpas
they will not hear the Buddha's name,
nor will they hear the correct Law—
such people are difficult to save.
For these reasons, Shariputra,
I have for their sake established expedient means,
preaching the way that ends all suffering,
and showing them nirvana.
But although I preach nirvana,
this is not a true extinction.
All phenomena from the very first
have of themselves constantly borne the marks of
     tranquil extinction.
Once the sons of the Buddha have carried out this path,
then in a future existence they will be able to become Buddhas.
I have employed the power of expedient means
to unfold and demonstrate this doctrine of three vehicles,
but the World-Honored Ones, every one of them,
all preach the single vehicle way.
Now before this great assembly
I must clear away all doubts and perplexities.
There is no discrepancy in the words of the Buddhas,
there is only the one vehicle, not two.
For numberless kalpas in the past
countless Buddhas who have now entered extinction,
a hundred, thousand, ten thousand, million types
in numbers incapable of calculation—

2. Sixty-two possible views that arise from the two views that there is existence and
that there is no existence. The term is often used to refer to all the non-Buddhist views
that were current in Shakyamuni's time.

such World-Honored Ones,
using different types of causes, similes, and parables,
the power of countless expedient means,
have expounded the characteristics of teachings.
These World-Honored Ones
have all preached the doctrine of the single vehicle,
converting countless living beings
and causing them to enter the Buddha way.
And these great sage lords,
knowing what is desired deep in the minds
of the heavenly and human beings and the other living things
throughout all the worlds,
have employed still other expedient means
to help illuminate the highest truth.
If there are living beings
who have encountered these past Buddhas,
and if they have listened to their Law, presented alms,
or kept the precepts, shown forbearance,
been assiduous, practiced meditation and wisdom, and so forth,
cultivating various kinds of merit and virtue,
then persons such as these
all have attained the Buddha way.
After the Buddhas have passed into extinction,
if persons are of good and gentle mind,
then living beings such as these
have all attained the Buddha way.
After the Buddhas have passed into extinction,
if persons make offerings to the relics,
raising ten thousand or a million kinds of towers,
using gold, silver and crystal,
seashell and agate,
carnelian, lapis lazuli, pearls
to purify and adorn them extensively,
in this way erecting towers;
or if they raise up stone mortuary temples
or those of sandalwood or aloes,
hovenia or other kinds of timber,
or of brick, tile, clay or earth;

if in the midst of the broad fields
they pile up earth to make a mortuary temple for the Buddhas,
or even if little boys at play
should collect sand to make a Buddha tower,
then persons such as these
have all attained the Buddha way.
If there are persons who for the sake of the Buddha
fashion and set up images,
carving them with many distinguishing characteristics,
then all have attained the Buddha way.
Or if they make things out of the seven kinds of gems,
of copper, red or white copper,
pewter, lead, tin,
iron, wood, or clay,
or use cloth soaked in lacquer or resin
to adorn and fashion Buddha images,
then persons such as these
have all attained the Buddha way.
If they employ pigments to paint Buddha images,
endowing them with the characteristics of hundredfold merit,
if they make them themselves or have others make them,
then all have attained the Buddha way.
Even if little boys in play
should use a piece of grass or wood or a brush,
or perhaps a fingernail
to draw an image of the Buddha,
such persons as these
bit by bit will pile up merit
and will become fully endowed with a mind of
    great compassion;
they all have attained the Buddha way.
Merely by converting the bodhisattvas
they bring salvation and release to numberless multitudes.
And if persons, in the presence of such memorial towers,
such jeweled images and painted images,
should with reverent minds make offerings
of flowers, incense, banners or canopies,
or if they should employ persons to make music,

striking drums or blowing horns or conch shells,
playing pipes, flutes, zithers, harps,
balloon guitars, cymbals and gongs,
and if these many kinds of wonderful notes
are intended wholly as an offering;
or if one with a joyful mind
sings a song in praise of the Buddha's virtue,
even if it is just one small note,
then all who do these things have attained the Buddha way.
If someone with a confused and distracted mind
should take even one flower
and offer it to a painted image,
in time he would come to see countless Buddhas.
Or if a person should bow or perform obeisance,
or should merely press his palms together,
or even should raise a single hand,
or give no more than a slight nod of the head,
and if this were done in offering to an image,
then in time he would come to see countless Buddhas.
And if he himself attains the unsurpassed way
and spreads salvation abroad to countless multitudes,
he will enter the nirvana of no remainder
as a fire dies out when the firewood is exhausted.
If persons with confused and distracted minds
should enter a memorial tower
and once exclaim, "Hail to the Buddha!"
then all have attained the Buddha way.
If from past Buddhas
when they were in the world or after their extinction,
there should be those who heard this Law,
then all have attained the Buddha way.
The World-Honored Ones of the future,
whose numbers will be incalculable,
these Thus Come Ones
will also employ expedient means to preach the Law,
and all these Thus Come Ones
through countless expedient means
will save and bring release to living beings

so that they enter the Buddha's wisdom which is free
    of outflows.
If there are those who hear the Law,
then not a one will fail to attain Buddhahood.
The original vow of the Buddhas
was that the Buddha way, which they themselves practice,
should be shared universally among living beings
so that they too may attain this same way.
The Buddhas of future ages,
although they preach hundreds, thousands, millions,
a countless number of doctrines,
in truth do so for the sake of the single vehicle.
The Buddhas, most honored of two-legged beings,
know that phenomena have no constantly fixed nature,
that the seeds of Buddhahood sprout through causation,
and for this reason they preach the single vehicle.
But that these phenomena are part of an abiding Law,
that the characteristics of the world are constantly abiding—
this they have come to know in the place of practice,
and as leaders and teachers they preach expedient means.
The presently existing Buddhas of the ten directions,
whom heavenly and human beings make offerings to,
who in number are like Ganges sands,
they have appeared in the world
in order to bring peace and comfort to living beings,
and they too preach the Law in this way.
They understand the foremost truth of tranquil extinction
and therefore employ the power of expedient means,
and though they point out various different paths,
in truth they do so for the sake of the Buddha vehicle.
They understand the actions of living beings,
the thoughts that lie deep in their minds,
the deeds they have carried out in the past,
their desires, their nature, the power of their exertions,
and whether their capacities are acute or dull,
and so they employ various causes and conditions,
similes, parables, and other words and phrases,
adapting what expedient means are suitable to their preaching.

Now I too am like this;
in order to bring peace and comfort to living beings
I employ various different doctrines
to disseminate the Buddha way.
Through the power of my wisdom
I know the nature and desires of living beings
and through expedient means I preach these doctrines,
causing all living beings to attain joy and gladness.
Shariputra, you should understand
that I view things through the Buddha eye,
I see the living beings in the six paths,
how poor and distressed they are, without merit or wisdom,
how they enter the perilous road of birth and death,
their sufferings continuing with never a break,
how deeply they are attached to the five desires,
like a yak enamored of its tail,
blinding themselves with greed and infatuation,
their vision so impaired they can see nothing.
They do not seek the Buddha, with his great might,
or the Law that can end their sufferings,
but enter deeply into erroneous views,
hoping to shed suffering through greater suffering.
For the sake of these living beings
I summon up a mind of great compassion.
When I first sat in the place of practice
and gazed at the tree and walked around it,
for the space of three times seven days
I pondered the matter in this way.
The wisdom I have attained, I thought,
is subtle, wonderful, the foremost.
But living beings, dull in capacity,
are addicted to pleasure and blinded by stupidity.
With persons such as this,
what can I say, how can I save them?
At that time the Brahma kings,
along with the heavenly king Shakra,
the Four Heavenly Kings who guard the world,
and the heavenly king Great Freedom,

in company with the other heavenly beings
and their hundreds and thousands and ten thousands
    of followers,
reverently pressed their palms together and bowed,
begging me to turn the wheel of the Law.
Immediately I thought to myself
that if I merely praised the Buddha vehicle,
then the living beings, sunk in their suffering,
would be incapable of believing in this Law.
And because they rejected the Law and failed to believe in it,
they would fall into the three evil paths.
It would be better if I did not preach the Law
but quickly entered into nirvana.
Then my thoughts turned to the Buddhas of the past
and the power of expedient means they had employed,
and I thought that the way I had now attained
should likewise be preached as three vehicles.
When I thought in this manner,
the Buddhas of the ten directions all appeared
and with brahma sounds comforted and instructed me.
"Well done, Shakyamuni!" they said.
"Foremost leader and teacher,
you have attained the unsurpassed Law.
But following the example of all other Buddhas,
you will employ the power of expedient means.
We too have all attained
the most wonderful, the foremost Law,
but for the sake of living beings
we make distinctions and preach the three vehicles.
People of small wisdom delight in a small Law,
unable to believe that they themselves could become Buddhas.
Therefore we employ expedient means,
making distinctions and preaching various goals.
But though we preach the three vehicles,
we do it merely in order to teach the bodhisattvas."
Shariputra, you should understand this.
When I heard these saintly lions
and their deep, pure, subtle, wonderful sounds,

I rejoiced, crying "Hail to the Buddhas!"
Then I thought to myself,
I have come into this impure and evil world,
and as these Buddhas have preached,
I too must follow that example in my actions.
After I had thought of the matter in this way,
I set out at once for Varanasi.
The marks of tranquil extinction borne by all phenomena
cannot be explained in words,
and therefore I used the power of expedient means
to preach to the five ascetics.
This I termed turning the wheel of the Law,
and also with regard to "the sound of nirvana,"
and "arhat," "Dharma" and "Samgha,"
I used these terms to indicate distinctions.
"From infinite kalpas in the past
I have extolled and taught the Law of nirvana,
ending the long sufferings of birth and death."
This is how I customarily preached.
Shariputra, you should know this.
When I looked at the Buddha sons,
I saw incalculable thousands, ten thousands, millions
who had determined to seek the way of the Buddha,
every one with a respectful and reverent mind,
all coming to the place of the Buddha,
persons who in the past had listened to other Buddhas
and heard the Law preached through expedient means.
Immediately the thought came to me
that the reason the Thus Come One has appeared
is so he may preach the Buddha wisdom.
Now is precisely the time to do so.
Shariputra, you should understand
that persons of dull capacity and small wisdom,
who are attached to appearances, proud and overbearing,
are incapable of believing in this Law.
Now I, joyful and fearless,
in the midst of the bodhisattvas,
honestly discarding expedient means,

will preach only the unsurpassed way.
When the bodhisattvas hear this Law,
they will be released from all entanglements of doubt.
The twelve hundred arhats,
they too will all attain Buddhahood.
Following the same fashion that the Buddhas of the
    three existences
employ in preaching the Law,
I now will do likewise,
preaching a Law that is without distinctions.
The times when the Buddhas appear in the world
are far apart and difficult to encounter.
And even when they appear in the world
it is difficult for them to preach this Law.
Throughout incalculable, innumerable kalpas
it is rare that one may hear this Law,
and a person capable of listening to this Law,
such a person is likewise rare.
It is like the udumbara flower
which all the world loves and delights in,
which heavenly and human beings look on as something rare,
but which appears only once in many many ages.
If a person hears this Law, delights and praises it,
even if he utters just one word,
then he has made offerings
to all the Buddhas of the three existences.
But a person like this is very rarely found,
rarer than the udumbara flower.
You should have no doubts.
I, being king of the doctrines,
make this announcement to the entire great assembly.
I employ only the single vehicle way
to teach and convert the bodhisattvas,
I have no voice-hearer disciples.
You, Shariputra,
and the voice-hearers and bodhisattvas,
you should understand that this wonderful Law
is the secret crux of the Buddhas.

In this evil world of the five impurities
those who merely delight in and are attached to the desires,
living beings such as this
in the end will never seek the Buddha way.
When evil persons in ages to come
hear the Buddha preach the single vehicle,
they will be confused, will not believe or accept it,
will reject the Law and fall into the evil paths.
But when there are those with a sense of shame, persons
   of purity
who have determined to seek the Buddha way,
then for the sake of such as these
one should widely praise the way of the single vehicle.
Shariputra, you should understand this.
The Law of the Buddhas is like this.
Employing ten thousand, a million expedient means,
they accord with what is appropriate in preaching the Law.
Those who are not versed in the matter
cannot fully comprehend this.
But you and the others already know
how the Buddhas, the teachers of the world,
accord with what is appropriate in employing expedient means.
You will have no more doubts or perplexities
but, your minds filled with great joy,
will know that you yourselves will attain Buddhahood.

3

SIMILE AND PARABLE

At that time Shariputra's mind danced with joy. Then he immediately stood up, pressed his palms together, gazed up in reverence at the face of the Honored One, and said to the Buddha, "Just now, when I heard from the World-Honored One this voice of the Law, my mind seemed to dance and I gained what I had never had before. Why do I say this? Because in the past when I heard a Law of this kind from the Buddha and saw how the bodhisattvas received prophecies that in time they would attain Buddhahood, I and the others felt that we had no part in the affair. We were deeply grieved to think we would never gain the immeasurable insight of the Thus Come One.

"World-Honored One, I have constantly lived in the mountain

forest or alone under the trees, sometimes sitting, sometimes walking around, and always I have thought to myself, Since I and the others all alike have entered into the nature of the Law, why does the Thus Come One use the Law of the Lesser Vehicle to bring us salvation?

"But the fault is ours, not that of the World-Honored One. Why do I say this? If we had been willing to wait until the true means for attaining anuttara-samyak-sambodhi was preached, then we would surely have obtained release through the Great Vehicle. But we failed to understand that the Buddha was employing expedient means and preaching what was appropriate to the circumstances. So when we first heard the Law of the Buddha, we immediately believed and accepted it, supposing that we had gained understanding.

"World-Honored One, for a long time now, all day and throughout the night, I have repeatedly taxed myself with this thought. But now I have heard from the Buddha what I had never heard before, a Law never known in the past, and it has ended all my doubts and regrets. My body and mind are at ease and I have gained a wonderful feeling of peace and security. Today at last I understand that truly I am the Buddha's son, born from the Buddha's mouth, born through conversion to the Law, gaining my share of the Buddha's Law!"

At that time Shariputra, wishing to state his meaning once more, spoke in verse form, saying:

> When I heard the sound of this Law,
> I gained what I had never had before.
> My mind was filled with great joy,
> I was released from all bonds of the net of doubt.
> From past times I have received the Buddha's teachings
> and have not been denied the Great Vehicle.
> The Buddha's sound is very rarely heard,
> but it can free living beings from distress.
> Already I have put an end to outflows,
> and hearing this, am freed from care and distress.
> I lived in the mountain valleys
> or under the forest trees,
> sometimes sitting, sometimes walking around,
> and constantly I thought of this matter—
> how severely I taxed myself!

"Why have I been deceived?" I said.
"I and the others are sons of the Buddha too,
all alike have entered the Law that is without outflows,
yet in times to come we will never be able
to expound the unsurpassed way.
The golden body, the thirty-two features,
the ten powers, the various emancipations—
though all alike share a single Law,
these we will never attain!
The eighty types of wonderful characteristics,
the eighteen unshared properties—
merits such as these
are all lost to us!"
When I was walking around alone,
I saw the Buddha among the great assembly,
his fame filling the ten directions,
bringing benefit far and wide to living beings,
and I thought to myself, I am deprived of such benefits!
How greatly have I been deceived!
Constantly, day and night,
whenever I pondered over this,
I wanted to ask the World-Honored One
whether I had indeed been deprived or not.
Constantly, when I saw the World-Honored One
praising the bodhisattvas,
then day and night
I would mull this matter over.
But now as I listen to the voice of the Buddha,
I see he preaches the Law in accordance with what
    is appropriate,
using this hard-to-conceive doctrine of no outflows
to lead people to the place of practice.
Formerly I was attached to erroneous views,
acting as teacher to the Brahmans.
But the World-Honored One, knowing what was in my mind,
rooted out my errors and preached nirvana.
I was freed of all my errors
and gained understanding of the Law of emptiness.

At that time my mind told me
I had reached the stage of extinction,
but now I realize
that that was not true extinction.
If the time should come when I can become a Buddha,
then I will possess all the thirty-two features
and heavenly and human beings, the many yakshas,
dragons, spirits and others will hold me in reverence.
When that time comes, then I can say
that at last all has been wiped out without residue.
In the midst of the great assembly, the Buddha
declared that I will become a Buddha.
When I heard the sound of this Law
my doubts and regrets were all wiped away.
At first, when I heard the Buddha's preaching,
there was great astonishment and doubt in my mind.
Is this not a devil pretending to be the Buddha,
trying to vex and confuse my mind? I thought.
But the Buddha employed various causes,
similes, and parables, expounding eloquently.
His mind was peaceful as the sea,
and as I listened, I was freed from the net of doubt.
The Buddha said that in past ages
the countless Buddhas who have passed into extinction
rested and abided in the midst of expedient means,
and all likewise preached this Law.
The Buddhas of the present and future,
whose numbers are beyond calculation,
they too will use expedient means
in expounding this same Law.
Thus the present World-Honored One,
being born and later leaving his family,
attaining the way and turning the wheel of the Law,
likewise employs expedient means in preaching.
The World-Honored One preaches the true way.
Papiyas would not do that.
Therefore I know for certain

this is not a devil pretending to be the Buddha.
But because I fell into the net of doubt
I supposed this to be the devil's work.
Now I hear the Buddha's soft and gentle sound,
profound, far-reaching, very subtle and wonderful,
expounding and discoursing on the pure Law,
and my mind is filled with great joy.
My doubts and regrets are forever ended,
I will rest and abide in true wisdom.
I am certain I will become a Buddha,
to be revered by heavenly and human beings,
turning the wheel of the unsurpassed Law
and teaching and converting the bodhisattvas.

At that time the Buddha said to Shariputra, "Now, in the midst of this great assembly of heavenly and human beings, shramanas, Brahmans and so forth, I say this. In the past, under twenty thousand million Buddhas, for the sake of the unsurpassed way I have constantly taught and converted you. And you throughout the long night followed me and accepted my instruction. Because I used expedient means to guide and lead you, you were born in the midst of my Law.

"Shariputra, in the past I taught you to aspire and vow to achieve the Buddha way. But now you have forgotten all that and instead suppose that you have already attained extinction. Now, because I want to make you recall to mind the way that you originally vowed to follow, for the sake of the voice-hearers I am preaching this Great Vehicle sutra called the Lotus of the Wonderful Law, a Law to instruct the bodhisattvas, one that is guarded and kept in mind by the Buddhas.

"Shariputra, in ages to come, after a countless, boundless, inconceivable number of kalpas have passed, you will make offerings to some thousands, ten thousands, millions of Buddhas, and will honor and uphold the correct Law. You will fulfill every aspect of the way of the bodhisattva and will be able to become a Buddha with the name Flower Glow Thus Come One, worthy of offerings, of right and universal knowledge, perfect clarity and conduct, well gone, understanding the world, unexcelled worthy, trainer of people, teacher of heavenly and human beings, Buddha, World-Honored One.

"Your realm will be called Free from Stain, the land will be level and smooth, pure and beautifully adorned, peaceful, bountiful and happy. Heavenly and human beings will flourish there. The ground will be of lapis lazuli, roads will crisscross it in eight directions, and ropes of gold will mark their boundaries. Beside each road will grow rows of seven-jeweled trees which will constantly flower and bear fruit. And this Flower Glow Thus Come One will employ the three vehicles to teach and convert living beings.

"Shariputra, when this Buddha appears, although it will not be an evil age, because of his original vow he will preach the Law through the three vehicles. His kalpa will be called Great Treasure Adornment. Why will it be called Great Treasure Adornment? Because in that land bodhisattvas will be looked on as a great treasure. Those bodhisattvas will be countless, boundless, inconceivable in number, beyond the reach of reckoning or of simile and parable. Without the power of Buddha wisdom, one cannot understand how many. Whenever these bodhisattvas wish to walk anywhere, jeweled flowers will uphold their feet.

"These bodhisattvas will not have just conceived the desire for enlightenment, but all will have spent a long time planting the roots of virtue. Under countless hundreds, thousands, tens of thousands, millions of Buddhas they will have carried out brahma practices in a flawless manner, and will have been perpetually praised by the Buddhas. Constantly they will have cultivated Buddha wisdom, acquiring great transcendental powers and thoroughly understanding the gateways to all the doctrines. They will be upright in character, without duplicity, firm in intent and thought. Bodhisattvas such as this will abound in that land.

"Shariputra, the life span of the Buddha Flower Glow will be twelve small kalpas, not counting the time when he is still a prince and before he becomes a Buddha. The people of his land will have a life span of eight small kalpas. When Flower Glow Thus Come One has lived for twelve small kalpas, he will prophesy that the bodhisattva Firm Full will attain anuttara-samyak-sambodhi. He will announce to the monks, 'This bodhisattva Firm Full will be the next to become a Buddha. He will be named Flower Feet Safely Walking, tathagata, arhat, samyak-sambuddha. His Buddha land will be like mine.'

"Shariputra, after the Buddha Flower Glow has passed into extinction, the era of the Correct Law will last for thirty-two small kalpas, and the era of the Counterfeit Law will last for another thirty-two small kalpas."

At that time the World-Honored One, wishing to state his meaning once more, spoke in verse form, saying:

> Shariputra, in ages to come
> you will become a Buddha, of universal wisdom, venerable,
> bearing the name Flower Glow,
> and you will save countless multitudes.
> You will make offerings to numberless Buddhas,
> be endowed with all the bodhisattva practices,
> the ten powers and other blessings,
> and will realize the unsurpassed way.
> After countless kalpas have passed,
> your kalpa will be named Great Treasure Adornment.
> Your world will be called Free from Stain,
> pure, without flaw or defilement.
> Its land will be made of lapis lazuli,
> its roads bounded by ropes of gold,
> and seven-jeweled trees in a jumble of colors
> will constantly bear blossoms and fruit.
> The bodhisattvas of that realm
> will always be firm in intent and thought.
> Transcendental powers and paramitas—
> each will be endowed with all of these,
> and under numberless Buddhas
> they will diligently study the bodhisattva way.
> Thus these great men
> will be converted by the Buddha Flower Glow.
> When that Buddha was still a prince,
> he gave up his country, abandoned worldly glory,
> and in his final incarnation
> left his family and attained the Buddha way.
> Flower Glow Buddha will continue in the world
> for a life span of twelve small kalpas.

The numerous people of his land
will have a life span of eight small kalpas.
After that Buddha has passed into extinction,
the Correct Law will endure in the world
for thirty-two small kalpas,
saving living beings far and wide.
When the Correct Law has passed away,
the Counterfeit Law will endure for thirty-two kalpas.
The Buddha's relics will circulate widely;
heavenly and human beings everywhere will make offerings
　　to them.
The actions of Flower Glow Buddha
will all be as I have said.
This most saintly and venerable of two-legged beings
will be foremost and without peer.
And he will be none other than you—
you should rejoice and count yourself fortunate!

At that time, when the four kinds of believers, namely, monks, nuns, laymen and laywomen, and the heavenly beings, dragons, yakshas, gandharvas, asuras, garudas, kimnaras, mahoragas, and others in the great assembly saw how Shariputra received from the Buddha this prophecy that he would attain anuttara-samyak-sambodhi, their hearts were filled with great joy and danced without end. Each one removed the upper robe that he or she was wearing and presented it as an offering to the Buddha. Shakra Devanam Indra, King Brahma, and the countless sons of gods likewise took their wonderful heavenly robes, heavenly mandarava flowers and great mandarava flowers and offered them to the Buddha. The heavenly robes they had scattered remained suspended in the air and turned round and round of themselves. Heavenly beings made music, a hundred, a thousand, ten thousand varieties, all at the same time in the midst of the air, raining down quantities of heavenly flowers and speaking these words: "In the past at Varanasi the Buddha first turned the wheel of the Law. Now he turns the wheel again, the wheel of the unsurpassed, the greatest Law of all!"

At that time the sons of gods, wishing to state their meaning once more, spoke in verse form, saying:

In the past at Varanasi
you turned the wheel of the Law of the four noble truths,
making distinctions, preaching that all things
are born and become extinct, being made up of the
   five components.
Now you turn the wheel of the most wonderful,
the unsurpassed great Law.
This Law is very profound and abstruse;
there are few who can believe it.
Since times past often we have heard
the World-Honored One's preaching,
but we have never heard
this kind of profound, wonderful and superior Law.
Since the World-Honored One preaches this Law,
we all welcome it with joy.
Shariputra with his great wisdom
has now received this venerable prophecy.
We too in the same way
will surely be able to attain Buddhahood,
throughout all the many worlds
the most venerable, the unsurpassed goal.
The Buddha way is difficult to fathom,
but you will preach with expedient means, according to what is
   appropriate.
The meritorious deeds we have done
in this existence or past existences,
and the blessings gained from seeing the Buddha—
all these we will apply to the Buddha way.

At that time Shariputra said to the Buddha: "World-Honored One, now I have no more doubts or regrets. In person I have received from the Buddha this prophecy that I will attain anuttara-samyak-sambodhi. These twelve hundred persons here whose minds are free—in the past they remained at the level of learning, and the Buddha constantly taught and converted them, saying, 'My Law can free you from birth, old age, sickness and death and enable you at last to achieve nirvana.' These persons, some of whom were still learning and some who had completed their learning, each believed that, because he had shed his views of 'self,' and also his views of 'existing' and 'not existing,' he had attained nirvana. But now from the World-Honored One they hear what they had never heard before, and all have fallen into doubt and perplexity.

"Very well, World-Honored One. I beg that for the sake of the four kinds of believers you will explain the causes and conditions and make it possible for them to shed their doubts and regrets."

At that time the Buddha said to Shariputra, "Did I not tell you earlier that when the Buddhas, the World-Honored Ones, cite various causes and conditions and use similes, parables, and other expressions, employing expedient means to preach the Law, it is all for the sake of anuttara-samyak-sambodhi? Whatever is preached is all for the sake of converting the bodhisattvas.

"Moreover, Shariputra, I too will now make use of similes and parables to further clarify this doctrine. For through similes and parables those who are wise can obtain understanding.

"Shariputra, suppose that in a certain town in a certain country there was a very rich man. He was far along in years and his wealth was beyond measure. He had many fields, houses and menservants. His own house was big and rambling, but it had only one gate. A great many people—a hundred, two hundred, perhaps as many as five hundred—lived in the house. The halls and rooms were old and decaying, the walls crumbling, the pillars rotten at their base, and the beams and rafters crooked and aslant.

"At that time a fire suddenly broke out on all sides, spreading through the rooms of the house. The sons of the rich man, ten, twenty, perhaps thirty, were inside the house. When the rich man saw the huge flames leaping up on every side, he was greatly alarmed and fearful and thought to himself, I can escape to safety through the flaming gate, but my sons are inside the burning house enjoying themselves and playing games, unaware, unknowing, without alarm or fear. The fire is closing in on them, suffering and pain threaten them, yet their minds have no sense of loathing or peril and they do not think of trying to escape!

"Shariputra, this rich man thought to himself, I have strength in my body and arms. I can wrap them in a robe or place them on a bench and carry them out of the house. And then again he thought, This house has only one gate, and moreover it is narrow and small.

My sons are very young, they have no understanding, and they love their games, being so engrossed in them that they are likely to be burned in the fire. I must explain to them why I am fearful and alarmed. The house is already in flames and I must get them out quickly and not let them be burned up in the fire!

"Having thought in this way, he followed his plan and called to all his sons, saying, 'You must come out at once!' But though the father was moved by pity and gave good words of instruction, the sons were absorbed in their games and unwilling to heed him. They had no alarm, no fright, and in the end no mind to leave the house. Moreover, they did not understand what the fire was, what the house was, what danger was. They merely raced about this way and that in play and looked at their father without heeding him.

"At that time the rich man had this thought: The house is already in flames from this huge fire. If I and my sons do not get out at once, we are certain to be burned. I must now invent some expedient means that will make it possible for the children to escape harm.

"The father understood his sons and knew what various toys and curious objects each child customarily liked and what would delight them. And so he said to them, 'The kind of playthings you like are rare and hard to find. If you do not take them when you can, you will surely regret it later. For example, things like these goat-carts, deer-carts, and ox-carts. They are outside the gate now where you can play with them. So you must come out of this burning house at once. Then whatever ones you want, I will give them all to you!'

"At that time, when the sons heard their father telling them about these rare playthings, because such things were just what they had wanted, each felt emboldened in heart and, pushing and shoving one another, they all came wildly dashing out of the burning house.

"At this time the rich man, seeing that his sons had gotten out safely and all were seated on the open ground at the crossroads and were no longer in danger, was greatly relieved and his mind danced for joy. At that time each of the sons said to his father, 'The playthings you promised us earlier, the goat-carts and deer-carts and ox-carts— please give them to us now!'

"Shariputra, at that time the rich man gave to each of his sons a large carriage of uniform size and quality. The carriages were tall and spacious and adorned with numerous jewels. A railing ran all around them and bells hung from all four sides. A canopy was stretched over the top, which was also decorated with an assortment of precious jewels. Ropes of jewels twined around, a fringe of flowers hung down, and layers of cushions were spread inside, on which were placed vermilion pillows. Each carriage was drawn by a white ox, pure and clean in hide, handsome in form and of great strength, capable of pulling the carriage smoothly and properly at a pace fast as the wind. In addition, there were many grooms and servants to attend and guard the carriage.

"What was the reason for this? This rich man's wealth was limitless and he had many kinds of storehouses that were all filled and overflowing. And he thought to himself, There is no end to my possessions. It would not be right if I were to give my sons small carriages of inferior make. These little boys are all my sons and I love them without partiality. I have countless numbers of large carriages adorned with seven kinds of gems. I should be fair-minded and give one to each of my sons. I should not show any discrimination. Why? Because even if I distributed these possessions of mine to every person in the whole country I would still not exhaust them, much less could I do so by giving them to my sons!

"At that time each of the sons mounted his large carriage, gaining something he had never had before, something he had originally never expected. Shariputra, what do you think of this? When this rich man impartially handed out to his sons these big carriages adorned with rare jewels, was he guilty of falsehood or not?"

Shariputra said, "No, World-Honored One. This rich man simply made it possible for his sons to escape the peril of fire and preserve their lives. He did not commit a falsehood. Why do I say this? Because if they were able to preserve their lives, then they had already obtained a plaything of sorts. And how much more so when, through an expedient means, they are rescued from that burning house! World-Honored One, even if the rich man had not given them the tiniest carriage, he would still not be guilty of falsehood. Why? Because this rich man had earlier made up his mind that he would employ an expedient means to cause his sons to escape. Using a device of this kind was no act of falsehood. How much less so, then, when the rich man knew that his wealth was limitless and he intended to enrich and benefit his sons by giving each of them a large carriage."

The Buddha said to Shariputra, "Very good, very good. It is just as you have said. And Shariputra, the Thus Come One is like this. That is, he is a father to all the world. His fears, cares and anxieties, ignorance and misunderstanding, have long come to an end, leaving no residue. He has fully succeeded in acquiring measureless insight, power and freedom from fear and gaining great supernatural powers and the power of wisdom. He is endowed with expedient means and the paramita of wisdom, his great pity and great compassion are constant and unflagging; at all times he seeks what is good and will bring benefit to all.

"He is born into the threefold world, a burning house, rotten and old, in order to save living beings from the fires of birth, old age, sickness and death, care, suffering, stupidity, misunderstanding, and the three poisons; to teach and convert them and enable them to attain anuttara-samyak-sambodhi.

"He sees living beings seared and consumed by birth, old age, sickness and death, care and suffering, sees them undergo many kinds of pain because of the five desires and the desire for wealth and profit. Again, because of their greed and attachment and striving they undergo numerous pains in their present existence, and later they undergo the pain of being reborn in hell or as beasts or hungry spirits. Even if they are reborn in the heavenly realm or the realm of human beings, they undergo the pain of poverty and want, the pain of parting from loved ones, the pain of encountering those they detest—all these many different kinds of pain.

"Yet living beings, drowned in the midst of all this, delight and amuse themselves, unaware, unknowing, without alarm or fear. They feel no sense of loathing and make no attempt to escape. In this burning house which is the threefold world, they race about to east and west, and though they encounter great pain, they are not distressed by it.

"Shariputra, when the Buddha sees this, then he thinks to himself, I am the father of living beings and I should rescue them from their sufferings and give them the joy of the measureless and boundless Buddha wisdom so that they may find their enjoyment in that.

"Shariputra, the Thus Come One also has this thought: If I should merely employ supernatural powers and the power of wisdom; if I should set aside expedient means and for the sake of living beings should praise the Thus Come One's insight, power and freedom from fear, then living beings would not be able to gain salvation. Why? Because these living beings have not yet escaped from birth, old age, sickness, death, care and suffering, but are consumed by flames in the burning house that is the threefold world. How could they be able to understand the Buddha's wisdom?

"Shariputra, that rich man, though he had strength in his body and arms, did not use it. He merely employed a carefully contrived expedient means and thus was able to rescue his sons from the peril of the burning house, and afterward gave each of them a large carriage adorned with rare jewels. And the Thus Come One does the same. Though he possesses power and freedom from fear, he does not use these. He merely employs wisdom and expedient means to rescue living beings from the burning house of the threefold world, expounding to them the three vehicles, the vehicle of the voice-hearer, that of the pratyekabuddha, and that of the Buddha.

"He says to them, 'You must not be content to stay in this burning house of the threefold world! Do not be greedy for its coarse and shoddy forms, sounds, scents, tastes and sensations! If you become attached to them and learn to love them, you will be burned up! You must come out of this threefold world at once so that you can acquire the three vehicles, the vehicles of the voice-hearer, the pratyekabuddha and the Buddha. I promise you now that you will get them, and that promise will never prove false. You have only to apply yourselves with diligent effort!'

"The Thus Come One employs this expedient means to lure living beings into action. And then he says to them, 'You should understand that these doctrines of the three vehicles are all praised by the sages. They are free, without entanglements, leaving nothing further to depend upon or seek. Mount these three vehicles, gain roots that are without outflows, gain powers, awareness, the way, meditation, emancipation, samadhis, and then enjoy yourselves. You will gain the delight of immeasurable peace and safety.'

"Shariputra, if there are living beings who are inwardly wise in nature, and who attend the Buddha, the World-Honored One, hear the Law, believe and accept it, and put forth diligent effort, desiring to escape quickly from the threefold world and seeking to attain nirvana, they shall be called [those who ride] the vehicle of the voice-hearer.

They are like those sons who left the burning house in the hope of acquiring goat-carts.

"If there are living beings who attend the Buddha, the World-Honored One, hear the Law, believe and accept it, and put forth diligent effort, seeking wisdom that comes of itself, taking solitary delight in goodness and tranquility, and profoundly understanding the causes and conditions of all phenomena, they shall be called [those who ride] the vehicle of the pratyekabuddha. They are like the sons who left the burning house in the hope of acquiring deer-carts.

"If there are living beings who attend the Buddha, the World-Honored One, hear the Law, believe and accept it, and put forth diligent effort, seeking comprehensive wisdom, Buddha wisdom, wisdom that comes of itself, teacherless wisdom, the insight of the Thus Come One, powers and freedom from fear, who pity and comfort countless living beings, bring benefit to heavenly and human beings, and save them all, they shall be called [those who ride] the Great Vehicle. Because the bodhisattvas seek this vehicle, they are called mahasattvas. They are like the sons who left the burning house in the hope of acquiring ox-carts.

"Shariputra, that rich man, seeing that his sons had all gotten out of the burning house safely and were no longer threatened, recalled that his wealth was immeasurable and presented each of his sons with a large carriage. And the Thus Come One does likewise. He is the father of all living beings. When he sees that countless thousands of millions of living beings, through the gateway of the Buddha's teaching, can escape the pains of the threefold world, the fearful and perilous road, and gain the delights of nirvana, the Thus Come One at that time has this thought: I possess measureless, boundless wisdom, power, fearlessness, the storehouse of the Law of the Buddhas. These living beings are all my sons. I will give the Great Vehicle to all of them equally so that there will not be those who gain extinction by themselves, but that all may do so through the extinction of the Thus Come One.

"To all the living beings who have escaped from the threefold world he then gives the delightful gifts of the meditation, emancipation, and so forth, of the Buddhas. All these are uniform in characteristics, uniform in type, praised by the sages, capable of producing pure, wonderful, supreme delight.

"Shariputra, that rich man first used three types of carriages to entice his sons, but later he gave them just the large carriage adorned with jewels, the safest, most comfortable kind of all. Despite this, that rich man was not guilty of falsehood. The Thus Come One does the same, and he is without falsehood. First he preaches the three vehicles to attract and guide living beings, but later he employs just the Great Vehicle to save them. Why? The Thus Come One possesses measureless wisdom, power, freedom from fear, the storehouse of the Law. He is capable of giving to all living beings the Law of the Great Vehicle. But not all of them are capable of receiving it.

"Shariputra, for this reason you should understand that the Buddhas employ the power of expedient means. And because they do so, they make distinctions in the one Buddha vehicle and preach it as three."

The Buddha, wishing to state his meaning once more, spoke in verse form, saying:

> Suppose there was a rich man
> who had a large house.
> This house was very old,
> and decayed and dilapidated as well.
> The halls, though lofty, were in dangerous condition,
> the bases of the pillars had rotted,
> beams and rafters were slanting and askew,
> foundations and steps were crumbling.
> Walls were cracked and gaping
> and the plaster had fallen off of them.
> The roof thatch was in disrepair or missing,
> the tips of the eaves had dropped off.
> The fences surrounding it were crooked or collapsed
> and heaped rubbish was piled all around.
> Some five hundred persons
> lived in the house.
> Kites, owls, hawks, eagles,
> crows, magpies, doves, pigeons,
> lizards, snakes, vipers, scorpions,
> centipedes and millipedes,
> newts and ground beetles,

weasels, raccoon dogs, mice, rats,
hordes of evil creatures
scurried this way and that.
Places that stank of excrement
overflowed in streams of filth
where dung beetles and other creatures gathered.
Foxes, wolves and jackals
gnawed and trampled in the filth
or tore apart dead bodies,
scattering bones and flesh about.
Because of this, packs of dogs
came racing to the spot to snatch and tear,
driven by hunger and fear,
searching everywhere for food,
fighting, struggling, seizing,
baring their teeth, snarling and howling.
That house was fearful, frightening,
so altered was its aspect.
In every part of it
there were goblins and trolls,
yakshas and evil spirits
who feed on human flesh
or on poisonous creatures.
The various evil birds and beasts
bore offspring, hatched and nursed them,
each hiding and protecting its young,
but the yakshas outdid one another
in their haste to seize and eat them.
And when they had eaten their fill,
their evil hearts became fiercer than ever;
the sound of their wrangling and contention
was terrifying indeed.
Kumbhanda demons
crouched on clumps of earth
or leaped one or two feet
off the ground,
idling, wandering here and there,
amusing themselves according to their whim.

Sometimes they seized a dog by two of its legs
and beat it till it had lost its voice,
or planted their feet on the dog's neck,
terrifying it for their own delight.
Again there were demons
with large tall bodies,
naked in form, black and emaciated,
constantly living there,
who would cry out in loud ugly voices,
shouting and demanding food.
There were other demons
whose throats were like needles,
or still other demons
with heads like the head of an ox,
some feeding on human flesh,
others devouring dogs.
Their hair like tangled weeds,
cruel, baleful, ferocious,
driven by hunger and thirst,
they dashed about shrieking and howling.
The yakshas and starving spirits
and the various evil birds and beasts
hungrily pressed forward in all directions,
peering out at the windows.
Such were the perils of this house,
threats and terrors beyond measure.
This house, old and rotting,
belonged to a certain man
and that man had gone nearby
and had not been out for long
when a fire
suddenly broke out in the house.
In one moment from all four sides
the flames rose up in a mass.
Ridgepoles, beams, rafters, pillars
exploded with a roar, quivering, splitting,
broke in two and came tumbling down
as walls and partitions collapsed.

The various demons and spirits
lifted their voices in a great wail,
the hawks, eagles and other birds,
the kumbhanda demons,
were filled with panic and terror,
not knowing how to escape.
The evil beasts and poisonous creatures
hid in their holes and dens,
and the pishacha demons,
who were also living there,
because they had done so little that was good,
were oppressed by the flames
and attacked one another,
drinking blood and gobbling flesh.
The jackals and their like
were already dead by this time
and the larger of the evil beasts
vied in devouring them.
Foul smoke swirled and billowed up,
filling the house on every side.
The centipedes and millipedes,
the poisonous snakes and their kind,
scorched by the flames,
came scurrying out of their lairs,
whereupon the kumbhanda demons
pounced on them and ate them.
In addition, the starving spirits,
the fire raging about their heads,
hungry, thirsty, tormented by the heat,
raced this way and that in terror and confusion.
Such was the state of that house,
truly frightening and fearful;
malicious injury, the havoc of fire—
many ills, not just one, afflicted it.
At this time the owner of the house
was standing outside the gate
when he heard someone say,
"A while ago your various sons,

in order to play their games,
went inside the house.
They are very young and lack understanding
and will be wrapped up in their amusements."
When the rich man heard this,
he rushed in alarm into the burning house,
determined to rescue his sons
and keep them from being burned by the flames.
He urged his sons to heed him,
explaining the many dangers and perils,
the evil spirits and poisonous creatures,
the flames spreading all around,
the multitude of sufferings
that would follow one another without end,
the poisonous snakes, lizards and vipers,
as well as the many yakshas
and kumbhanda demons,
the jackals, foxes and dogs,
hawks, eagles, kites, owls,
ground beetles and similar creatures,
driven and tormented by hunger and thirst,
truly things to be feared.
His sons could not stay in such a perilous place,
much less when it was all on fire!
But the sons had no understanding
and though they heard their father's warnings,
they continued engrossed in their amusements,
never ceasing their games.
At that time the rich man
thought to himself:
My sons behave in this manner,
adding to my grief and anguish.
In this house at present
there is not a single joy,
and yet my sons,
wrapped up in their games,
refuse to heed my instructions
and will be destroyed by the fire!

Then it occurred to him
to devise some expedient means,
and he said to his sons,
"I have many kinds
of rare and marvelous toys,
wonderful jeweled carriages,
goat-carts, deer-carts,
carts drawn by big oxen.
They are outside the gate right now—
you must come out and see them!
I have fashioned these carts
explicitly for you.
You may enjoy whichever you choose,
play with them as you like!"
When the sons heard
this description of the carts,
at once they vied with one another
in dashing out of the house,
till they reached the open ground,
away from all peril and danger.
When the rich man saw that his sons
had escaped from the burning house
and were standing in the crossroads,
he seated himself on a lion seat,
congratulating himself in these words:
"Now I am content and happy.
These sons of mine
have been very difficult to raise.
Ignorant, youthful, without understanding,
they entered that perilous house
with its many poisonous creatures
and its goblins to be feared.
The roaring flames of the great fire
rose up on all four sides,
yet those sons of mine
still clung to their games.
But now I have saved them,
caused them to escape from danger.

That is the reason, good people,
I am content and happy."
At that time the sons,
seeing their father comfortably seated,
all went to where he was
and said to him:
"Please give us
the three kinds of jeweled carriages
you promised us earlier.
You said if we came out of the house
you'd give us three kinds of carts
and we could choose whichever we wished.
Now is the time
to give them to us!"
The rich man was very wealthy
and had many storehouses.
With gold, silver, lapis lazuli,
seashells, agate,
and other such precious things
he fashioned large carriages
beautifully adorned and decorated,
with railings running around them
and bells hanging from all sides.
Ropes of gold twisted and twined,
nets of pearls
stretched over the top,
and fringes of golden flowers
hung down everywhere.
Multicolored decorations
wound around and encircled the carriages,
soft silks and gauzes
served for cushions,
with fine felts of most wonderful make
valued at thousands or millions,
gleaming white and pure,
to spread over them.
There were large white oxen,
sleek, stalwart, of great strength,

handsome in form,
to draw the jeweled carriages,
and numerous grooms and attendants
to accompany and guard them.
These wonderful carriages
the man presented to each of his sons alike.
The sons at that time
danced for joy,
mounting the jeweled carriages,
driving off in all directions,
delighting and amusing themselves
freely and without hindrance.
I say this to you, Shariputra—
I am like this rich man.
I, most venerable of the sages,
am the father of this world
and all living beings
are my children.
But they are deeply attached to worldly pleasures
and lacking in minds of wisdom.
There is no safety in the threefold world;
it is like a burning house,
replete with a multitude of sufferings,
truly to be feared,
constantly beset with the griefs and pains
of birth, old age, sickness and death,
which are like fires
raging fiercely and without cease.
The Thus Come One has already left
the burning house of the threefold world
and dwells in tranquil quietude
in the safety of forest and plain.
But now this threefold world
is all my domain,
and the living beings in it
are all my children.
Now this place
is beset by many pains and trials.

I am the only person
who can rescue and protect others,
but though I teach and instruct them,
they do not believe or accept my teachings,
because, tainted by desires,
they are deeply immersed in greed and attachment.
So I employ an expedient means,
describing to them the three vehicles,
causing all living beings
to understand the pains of the threefold world,
and then I set forth and expound
a way whereby they can escape from the world.
If these children of mine
will only determine in their minds to do so,
they can acquire all the three understandings
and the six transcendental powers,
can become pratyekabuddhas
or bodhisattvas who never regress.
I say to you, Shariputra,
for the sake of living beings
I employ these similes and parables
to preach the single Buddha vehicle.
If you and the others are capable
of believing and accepting my words,
then all of you are certain
to attain the Buddha way.
This vehicle is subtle, wonderful,
foremost in purity;
throughout all worlds
it stands unsurpassed.
The Buddha delights in and approves it,
and all living beings
should praise it,
offer it alms and obeisance.
There are immeasurable thousands of millions
of powers, emancipations,
meditations, wisdoms,
and other attributes of the Buddha.

But if the children can obtain this vehicle,
it will allow them
day and night for unnumbered kalpas
to find constant enjoyment,
to join the bodhisattvas
and the multitude of voice-hearers
in mounting this jeweled vehicle
and proceeding directly to the place of practice.
For these reasons,
though one should seek diligently in the ten directions,
he will find no other vehicles
except when the Buddha preaches them as an expedient means.
I tell you, Shariputra,
you and the others
are all my children,
and I am a father to you.
For repeated kalpas
you have burned in the flames of manifold sufferings,
but I will save you all
and cause you to escape from the threefold world.
Although earlier I told you
that you had attained extinction,
that was only the end of birth and death,
it was not true extinction.
Now what is needed
is simply that you acquire Buddha wisdom.
If there are bodhisattvas
here in this assembly,
let them with a single mind
listen to the true Law of the Buddhas.
Though the Buddhas, the World-Honored Ones,
employ expedient means,
the living beings converted by them
are all bodhisattvas.
If there are persons of little wisdom
who are deeply attached to love and desire,
because they are that way,
the Buddha preaches for them the rule of suffering.

Then the living beings will be glad in mind,
having gained what they never had before.
The rule of suffering which the Buddha preaches
is true and never varies.
If there are living beings
who do not understand the root of suffering,
who are deeply attached to the causes of suffering
and cannot for a moment put them aside,
because they are that way,
the Buddha uses expedient means to preach the way.
As to the cause of all suffering,
it has its root in greed and desire.
If greed and desire are wiped out,
it will have no place to dwell.
To wipe out all suffering—
this is called the third rule.
For the sake of this rule, the rule of extinction,
one practices the way.
And when one escapes from the bonds of suffering,
this is called attaining emancipation.
By what means
can a person attain emancipation?
Separating oneself from falsehood and delusion—
this alone may be called emancipation.
But if a person has not truly
been able to emancipate himself from everything,
then the Buddha will say
he has not achieved true extinction,
because such a person
has not yet gained the unsurpassed way.
My purpose is not to try
to cause them to reach extinction.
I am the Dharma King,
free to do as I will with the Law.
To bring peace and safety to living beings—
that is the reason I appear in the world.
I say to you, Shariputra,
this Dharma seal of mine

I preach because I wish
to bring benefit to the world.
You must not recklessly transmit it
wherever you happen to wander.
If there is someone who hears it,
responds with joy and gratefully accepts it,
you should know that that person
is an avivartika.
If there is someone who believes and accepts
the Law of this sutra,
that person has already seen
the Buddhas of the past,
has respectfully offered alms to them
and listened to this Law.
If there is someone who can
believe what you preach,
then that person has seen me,
and has also seen you
and the other monks
and the bodhisattvas.
This Lotus Sutra
is preached for those with profound wisdom.
If persons of shallow understanding hear it,
they will be perplexed and fail to comprehend.
As for all the voice-hearers
and pratyekabuddhas,
in this sutra there are things
that are beyond their powers.
Even you, Shariputra,
in the case of this sutra
were able to gain entrance through faith alone.
How much more so, then, the other voice-hearers.
Those other voice-hearers—
it is because they have faith in the Buddha's words
that they can comply with this sutra,
not because of any wisdom of their own.
Also, Shariputra,
to persons who are arrogant or lazy

or taken up with views of the self,
do not preach this sutra.
Those with the shallow understanding of ordinary persons,
who are deeply attached to the five desires,
cannot comprehend it when they hear it.
Do not preach it to them.
If a person fails to have faith
but instead slanders this sutra,
immediately he will destroy all the seeds
for becoming a Buddha in this world.
Or perhaps he will scowl with knitted brows
and harbor doubt or perplexity.
Listen and I will tell you
the penalty this person must pay.
Whether the Buddha is in the world
or has already entered extinction,
if this person should slander
a sutra such as this,
or on seeing those who read, recite,
copy and uphold this sutra,
should despise, hate, envy,
or bear grudges against them,
the penalty this person must pay—
listen, I will tell you now:
When his life comes to an end
he will enter the Avichi hell,
be confined there for a whole kalpa,
and when the kalpa ends, be born there again.
He will keep repeating this cycle
for a countless number of kalpas.
Though he may emerge from hell,
he will fall into the realm of beasts,
becoming a dog or jackal,
his form lean and scruffy,
dark, discolored, with scabs and sores,
something for men to make sport of.
Or again he will be
hated and despised by men,

constantly plagued by hunger and thirst,
his bones and flesh dried up,
in life undergoing torment and hardship,
in death buried beneath tiles and stones.
Because he cut off the seeds of Buddhahood
he will suffer this penalty.
If he should become a camel
or be born in the shape of a donkey,
his body will constantly bear heavy burdens
and have the stick or whip laid on it.
He will think only of water and grass
and understand nothing else.
Because he slandered this sutra,
this is the punishment he will incur.
Or he will be born as a jackal
who comes to the village,
body all scabs and sores,
having only one eye,
by the boys
beaten and cuffed,
suffering grief and pain,
sometimes to the point of death.
And after he has died
he will be born again in the body of a serpent,
long and huge in size,
measuring five hundred yojanas,
deaf, witless, without feet,
slithering along on his belly,
with little creatures
biting and feeding on him,
day and night undergoing hardship,
never knowing rest.
Because he slandered this sutra,
this is the punishment he will incur.
If he should become a human being,
his faculties will be blighted and dull,
he will be puny, vile, bent, crippled,
blind, deaf, hunchbacked.

The things he says
people will not believe,
the breath from his mouth will be constantly foul,
he will be possessed by devils,
poor and lowly,
ordered around by others,
plagued by many ailments, thin and gaunt,
having no one to turn to.
Though he attached himself to others,
they would never think of him;
though he might gain something,
he would at once lose or forget it.
Though he might practice the art of medicine
and by its methods cure someone's disease,
the person would grow sicker from some other malady
and perhaps in the end would die.
If he himself had an illness,
no one would aid or nurse him,
and though he took good medicine,
it would only make his condition worse.
If others should turn against him,
he would find himself plundered and robbed.
His sins would be such
that they would bring unexpected disaster on him.
A sinful person of this sort
will never see the Buddha,
the king of the many sages,
preaching the Law, teaching and converting.
A sinful person of this sort
will constantly be born amid difficulties,
crazed, deaf, confused in mind,
and never will hear the Law.
For countless kalpas
numerous as Ganges sands
he will at birth become deaf and dumb,
his faculties impaired,
will constantly dwell in hell,
strolling in it as though it were a garden,

and the other evil paths of existence
he will look on as his own home.
Camel, donkey, pig, dog—
these will be the forms he will take on.
Because he slandered this sutra,
this is the punishment he will incur.
If he should become a human being,
he will be deaf, blind, dumb.
Poverty, want, all kinds of decay
will be his adornment;
water blisters, diabetes,
scabs, sores, ulcers,
maladies such as these
will be his garments.
His body will always smell bad,
filthy and impure.
Deeply attached to views of self,
he will grow in anger and hatred;
aflame with licentious desires,
he will not spurn even birds or beasts.
Because he slandered this sutra,
this is the punishment he will incur.
I tell you, Shariputra,
if I were to describe the punishments that fall
on persons who slander this sutra,
I could exhaust a kalpa and never come to the end.
For this reason
I expressly say to you,
do not preach this sutra
to persons who are without wisdom.
But if there are those of keen capacities,
wise and understanding,
of much learning and strong memory,
who seek the Buddha way,
then to persons such as this
it is permissible to preach it.
If there are persons who have seen
hundreds and thousands and millions of Buddhas,

have planted many good roots
and are firm and deeply committed in mind,
then to persons such as this
it is permissible to preach it.
If there are persons who are diligent,
constantly cultivating a compassionate mind,
not begrudging of life or limb,
then it is permissible to preach it.
If there are persons who are respectful, reverent,
with minds set on nothing else,
who separate themselves from common folly
to live alone among mountains and waters,
then to persons such as this
it is permissible to preach it.
Again, Shariputra,
if you see a person
who thrusts aside evil friends
and associates with good companions,
then to a person such as this
it is permissible to preach it.
If you see a son of the Buddha
observing the precepts, clean and spotless
as a pure bright gem,
seeking the Great Vehicle sutra,
then to a person such as this
it is permissible to preach it.
If a person is without anger,
upright and gentle in nature,
constantly pitying all beings,
respectful and reverent to the Buddhas,
then to a person such as this
it is permissible to preach it.
Again, if a son of the Buddha
in the midst of the great assembly
should with a pure mind
employ various causes and conditions,
similes, parables, and other expressions
to preach the Law in unhindered fashion,

to a person such as this
it is permissible to preach it.
If there are monks who,
for the sake of comprehensive wisdom,
seek the Law in every direction,
pressing palms together, gratefully accepting,
desiring only to accept and embrace
the sutra of the Great Vehicle
and not accepting a single verse
of the other sutras,
to persons such as this
it is permissible to preach it.
If a person, earnest in mind,
seeks this sutra
as though he were seeking the Buddha's relics,
and having gained and gratefully accepted it,
that person shows no intention
of seeking other sutras
and has never once given thought
to the writings of the non-Buddhist doctrines,
to a person such as this
it is permissible to preach it.
I tell you, Shariputra,
if I described all the characteristics
of those who seek the Buddha way,
I could exhaust a kalpa and never be done.
Persons of this type
are capable of believing and understanding.
Therefore for them you should preach
the Lotus Sutra of the Wonderful Law.

10

THE TEACHER
OF THE LAW

At that time the World-Honored One addressed Bodhisattva Medicine King, and through him the eighty thousand great men, saying: "Medicine King, do you see in this great assembly the immeasurable number of heavenly beings, dragon kings, yakshas, gandharvas, asuras, garudas, kimnaras, mahoragas, human and nonhuman beings, as well as monks, nuns, laymen and laywomen, those who seek to become voice-hearers, who seek to become pratyekabuddhas, or who seek the Buddha way? Upon these various kinds of beings who in the presence of the Buddha listen to one verse or one phrase of the Lotus Sutra of the Wonderful Law and for a moment think of it with joy I will bestow on all of them a prophecy that they will attain anuttara-samyak-sambodhi."

The Buddha said to Medicine King: "In addition, if after the Thus Come One has passed into extinction there should be someone who listens to the Lotus Sutra of the Wonderful Law, even one verse or one phrase, and for a moment thinks of it with joy, I will likewise bestow on him a prophecy that he will attain anuttara-samyak-sambodhi. Again if there are persons who embrace, read, recite, expound and copy the Lotus Sutra of the Wonderful Law, even only one verse, and look upon this sutra with the same reverence as they would the Buddha, presenting various offerings of flowers, incense, necklaces, powdered incense, paste incense, incense for burning, silken canopies, streamers and banners, clothing and music, and pressing their palms together in reverence, then, Medicine King, you should understand that such persons have already offered alms to a hundred thousand million Buddhas and in the place of the Buddhas have fulfilled their great vow, and because they take pity on living beings they have been born in this human world.

"Medicine King, if someone should ask what living beings will be able to attain Buddhahood in a latter-day existence, then you should show him that all these people in a latter-day existence are certain to attain Buddhahood. Why? Because if good men and good women embrace, read, recite, expound and copy the Lotus Sutra, even one phrase of it, offer various kinds of alms to the sutra, flowers, incense, necklaces, powdered incense, paste incense, incense for burning, silken canopies, streamers and banners, clothing and music, and press their palms together in reverence, then these persons will be looked up to and honored by all the world. Alms will be offered to them such as would be offered to the Thus Come One. You should understand that these persons are great bodhisattvas who have succeeded in attaining anuttara-samyak-sambodhi. Pitying living beings, they have vowed to be born among them where they may broadly expound and make distinctions regarding the Lotus Sutra of the Wonderful Law. How much more so is this true, then, of those who can embrace the entire sutra and offer various types of alms to it!

"Medicine King, you should understand that these persons voluntarily relinquish the reward due them for their pure deeds and, in the

time after I have passed into extinction, because they pity living beings, they are born in this evil world so they may broadly expound
this sutra. If one of these good men or good women in the time after
I have passed into extinction is able to secretly expound the Lotus
Sutra to one person, even one phrase of it, then you should know that
he or she is the envoy of the Thus Come One. He has been dispatched
by the Thus Come One and carries out the Thus Come One's work.
And how much more so those who in the midst of the great assembly
broadly expound the sutra for others!

"Medicine King, if there should be an evil person who, his mind
destitute of goodness, should for the space of a kalpa appear in the
presence of the Buddha and constantly curse and revile the Buddha,
that person's offense would still be rather light. But if there were a
person who spoke only one evil word to curse or defame the lay
persons or monks or nuns who read and recite the Lotus Sutra, then
his offense would be very grave.

"Medicine King, these persons who read and recite the Lotus Sutra—
you should understand that these persons adorn themselves with the
adornments of the Buddha; they are borne upon the shoulders of the
Thus Come One. Wherever they may go, one should greet them with
bows, with palms pressed single-mindedly together, with reverence
and alms, with respect and praise, flowers, incense, necklaces, powdered
incense, paste incense, incense for burning, silken canopies, streamers
and banners, clothing, delicacies and the making of music. The finest
alms that can be offered to a person should be offered to them. Heavenly treasures should be scattered over them, the treasure hoards of
heaven should be given them as gifts. Why do I say this? Because
these persons delight in expounding the Law. And if one listens to
them for even a moment, he will immediately attain the ultimate
anuttara-samyak-sambodhi."

At that time the World-Honored One, wishing to state his meaning
once more, spoke in verse form, saying:

> If you wish to abide in the Buddha way
> and successfully gain the wisdom that comes of itself,
> you should be constantly diligent in offering alms
> to those who embrace the Lotus Sutra.
> If you have a wish to quickly obtain

wisdom regarding all species of things,
you should embrace this sutra
and at the same time give alms to those who do so.
If one is capable of embracing
the Lotus Sutra of the Wonderful Law,
know that such a person is an envoy of the Buddha
who thinks with pity of living beings.
Those who are capable of embracing
the Lotus Sutra of the Wonderful Law
relinquish their claim to the pure land
and out of pity for living beings are born here.
Know that persons such as these
freely choose where they will be born,
and choose to be born in this evil world
so they may broadly expound the unsurpassed Law.
You should offer heavenly flowers and incense,
robes decked with heavenly treasures,
the wonderful treasure hoards of heaven
as alms to those who preach the Law.
In the evil world following my extinction
if there are those who can embrace this sutra,
you should press your palms together in reverence
and offer alms to them as you would to the
    World-Honored One.
The choicest delicacies, all that is sweet and tasty,
along with various types of clothing
you should offer as alms to these Buddha sons
in hopes you may hear a moment of their preaching.
If there are those in a later age
who can accept and embrace this sutra,
they are my envoys sent out among the people
to perform the Thus Come One's work.
If for the space of a kalpa
one should constantly harbor a mind destitute of good
and with angry looks should revile the Buddha,
he will be committing an offense of immeasurable gravity.
But if toward those who read, recite and embrace
this Lotus Sutra

one should even for a moment direct evil words,
his offense will be far greater.
If there is someone who seeks the Buddha way
and during a certain kalpa
presses palms together in my presence
and recites numberless verses of praise,
because of these praises of the Buddha
he will gain immeasurable blessings.
And if one lauds and extols those who uphold this sutra,
his good fortune will be even greater.
For the space of eighty million kalpas,
with the most wonderful shapes and sounds,
with that which is pleasing to smell, taste and touch,
offer alms to the upholders of this sutra!
If you have offered alms in this manner
and have heard the teachings for even a moment,
then you will experience joy and good fortune,
saying, "I have gained great benefit!"
Medicine King, now I say to you,
I have preached various sutras,
and among those sutras
the Lotus is the foremost!

At that time the Buddha spoke once more to the bodhisattva and mahasattva Medicine King, saying: "The sutras I have preached number immeasurable thousands, ten thousands, millions. Among the sutras I have preached, now preach, and will preach, this Lotus Sutra is the most difficult to believe and the most difficult to understand. Medicine King, this sutra is the storehouse of the secret crux of the Buddhas. It must not be distributed or recklessly transmitted to others. It has been guarded by the Buddhas, the World-Honored Ones, and from times past until now has never been openly expounded. And since hatred and jealousy toward this sutra abound even when the Thus Come One is in the world, how much more will this be so after his passing?

"Medicine King, you should know that after the Thus Come One has entered extinction, if there are those who can copy, uphold, read and recite this sutra, offer alms to it and expound if for others, then the Thus Come One will cover them with his robe, and they will also be protected and kept in mind by the Buddhas who are now present in other regions. Such persons possess the power of great faith, the power of aspiration, the power of good roots. You should know that such persons lodge in the same place as the Thus Come One, and the Thus Come One pats them on the head with his hand.

"Medicine King, in any place whatsoever where this sutra is preached, where it is read, where it is recited, where it is copied, or where a roll of it exists, in all such places there should be erected towers made of the seven kinds of gems, and they should be made very high and broad and well adorned. There is no need to enshrine the relics of the Buddha there. Why? Because in such towers the entire body of the Thus Come One is already present. All kinds of flowers, incense, necklaces, silken canopies, streamers and banners, music and hymns should be offered as alms to these towers and they should be accorded reverence, honor and praise. If when people see these towers they bow in obeisance and offer alms, then you should know that such persons have all drawn near to anuttara-samyak-sambodhi.

"Medicine King, though there may be many persons, those still living in the household and those who have left it, who practice the way of the bodhisattva, if they are not willing to see, hear, read, recite, copy, embrace and offer alms to this Lotus Sutra, then you should know that such persons are not yet practicing the bodhisattva way in a fitting manner. But if there are those who will listen to this sutra, then they are capable of practicing the bodhisattva way in a fitting manner. If among the living beings who seek the Buddha way there are those who see or hear this Lotus Sutra, and who, having heard it, believe, understand and embrace it, then you should know that these persons can draw near to anuttara-samyak-sambodhi.

"Medicine King, suppose there is a man who is parched with thirst and in need of water. On an upland plateau he begins digging a hole in search of water, but he sees that the soil is dry and knows that water is still far away. He does not cease his efforts, however, and bit by bit he sees the soil becoming damper, until gradually he has worked his way into mud. Now he is determined in his mind to go on, for he knows that he is bound to be nearing water.

"The way of the bodhisattva is the same as this. As long as a person has not yet heard, not yet understood, and not yet been able to practice this Lotus Sutra, then you should know that that person is still far away from anuttara-samyak-sambodhi. But if the person is able to hear, understand, ponder and practice the sutra, then you should know that he can draw near to anuttara-samyak-sambodhi. Why? Because all bodhisattvas who attain anuttara-samyak-sambodhi in all cases do so through this sutra. This sutra opens the gate of expedient means and shows the form of true reality. This storehouse of the Lotus Sutra is hidden deep and far away where no person can reach it. But now the Buddha, teaching, converting and leading to success the bodhisattvas, opens it up for them.

"Medicine King, if there are bodhisattvas who, on hearing this Lotus Sutra, respond with surprise, doubt and fear, then you should know that they are bodhisattvas who have only newly embarked on their course. And if there are voice-hearers who, on hearing this sutra, respond with surprise, doubt, and fear, then you should know that they are persons of overbearing arrogance.

"Medicine King, if there are good men and good women who, after the Thus Come One has entered extinction, wish to expound this Lotus Sutra for the four kinds of believers, how should they expound it? These good men and good women should enter the Thus Come One's room, put on the Thus Come One's robe, sit in the Thus Come One's seat, and then for the sake of the four kinds of believers broadly expound this sutra.

"The 'Thus Come One's room' is the state of mind that shows great pity and compassion toward all living beings. The 'Thus Come One's robe' is the mind that is gentle and forbearing. The 'Thus Come One's seat' is the emptiness of all phenomena. One should seat oneself comfortably therein and after that, with a mind never lazy or remiss, should for the sake of the bodhisattvas and the four kinds of believers broadly expound this Lotus Sutra.

"Medicine King, I will send persons conjured up by magic to other lands to gather together assemblies to listen to the Law. And I will also send monks, nuns, laymen and laywomen conjured up by magic to listen to the preaching of the Law. These persons conjured up by magic will listen to the Law, believe and accept it, and abide by it without violation. If the preachers of the Law are in an empty and silent place, I will at that time send large numbers of heavenly beings, dragons, spirits, gandharvas, asuras, and others to listen to their preaching of the Law. Though I should be in another land, from time to time I will make it possible for the preachers of the Law to see my body. If they should forget a phrase of this sutra, I will appear and prompt them so that they are able to recite the text correctly and in full."

At that time the World-Honored One, wishing to state his meaning once more, spoke in verse form, saying:

> If you wish to put aside all sloth and remissness,
> you must listen to this sutra.
> It is hard to get a chance to hear this sutra,
> and believing and accepting it too is hard.
> If a person is thirsty and wants water
> he may dig a hole in the high plateau,
> but as long as he sees that the soil is dry
> he knows that water is still far away.
> But bit by bit he sees the soil grow damp and muddy
> and then he knows for certain he is nearing water.
> Medicine King, you should understand
> that people are like this—
> if they do not hear the Lotus Sutra,
> they will be far removed from the Buddha's wisdom.
> But if they hear this profound sutra
> which defines the Law of the voice-hearer,
> if they hear this king of the sutras
> and afterward carefully ponder it,
> then you should know that such persons
> are close to the wisdom of the Buddha.
> If a person expounds this sutra,
> he should enter the Thus Come One's room,
> put on the Thus Come One's robe,
> sit in the Thus Come One's seat,
> confront the assembly without fear
> and broadly expound it for them, making distinctions.
> Great pity and compassion are the room,
> gentleness and patience are the robe,
> the emptiness of all phenomena is the seat,
> and from that position one should expound the Law for them.
> If when a person expounds this sutra

there is someone who speaks ill and reviles him
or attacks him with swords and staves, tiles and stones,
he should think of the Buddha and for that reason be patient.
In a thousand, ten thousand, a million lands
I will manifest my pure and durable body
and for immeasurable millions of kalpas
will expound the Law for living beings.
If after I have entered extinction
there are those who can expound this sutra,
I will send the four kinds of believers, magically conjured,
monks and nuns
and men and women of pure faith,
to offer alms to the teachers of the Law;
they will lead and guide living beings,
assemble them and cause them to listen to the Law.
If someone thinks to do evil to the preachers
with swords and staves or with tiles and stones,
I will dispatch persons magically conjured
who will act to guard and protect them.
If those who expound the Law
are alone in an empty and silent place,
and in that stillness where no human voice sounds
they read and recite this sutra,
at that time I will manifest
my pure and radiant body for them.
If they forget a passage or a phrase
I will prompt them so they will be thorough and effective.
If persons endowed with these virtues
should expound to the four kinds of believers
and read and recite the sutra in an empty place,
I will enable all of them to see my body.
And if the expounders are in an empty and silent place
I will send heavenly beings, dragon kings,
yakshas, spirits and others
to be an assembly and listen to the Law.
Persons such as this will delight in expounding the Law,
making distinctions and encountering no hindrance.
Because the Buddhas guard and keep them in mind,

they will be able to bring joy to the great assembly.
If one stays close to the teachers of the Law
he will speedily gain the bodhisattva way.
By following and learning from these teachers
he will see Buddhas as numerous as Ganges sands.

11

THE EMERGENCE OF
THE TREASURE TOWER

At that time in the Buddha's presence there was a tower adorned with the seven treasures, five hundred yojanas in height and two hundred and fifty yojanas in width and depth, that rose up out of the earth and stood suspended in the air. Various kinds of precious objects adorned it. It had five thousand railings, a thousand, ten thousand rooms, and numberless streamers and banners decorated it. Festoons of jewels hung down and ten thousand million jeweled bells were suspended from it. All four sides emitted a fragrance of tamalapatra and sandalwood that pervaded the whole world. Its banners and canopies were made of the seven treasures, namely, gold, silver, lapis lazuli, seashell, agate, pearl, and carnelian, and it was so high it reached to the heavenly palaces of the Four Heavenly Kings. The gods of the Trayastrimsha heaven rained down heavenly mandarava flowers as an offering to the treasure tower, and the other heavenly beings and the dragons, yakshas, gandharvas, asuras, garudas, kimnaras, mahoragas, human and nonhuman beings, an assembly of thousands, ten thousands, millions, offered all kinds of flowers, incense, necklaces, streamers, canopies and music as alms to the treasure tower, paying it reverence, honor and praise.

At that time a loud voice issued from the treasure tower, speaking words of praise: "Excellent, excellent! Shakyamuni, World-Honored One, that you can take the great wisdom of equality, a Law to instruct the bodhisattvas, guarded and kept in mind by the Buddhas, the Lotus Sutra of the Wonderful Law, and preach it for the sake of the great assembly! It is as you say, as you say. Shakyamuni, World-Honored One, all that you have expounded is the truth!"

At that time the four kinds of believers saw the great treasure tower suspended in the air, and they heard the voice that issued from the tower. All experienced the joy of the Law, marveling at this thing they had never known before. They rose from their seats, pressed their palms together in reverence, and then retired to one side.

At that time there was a bodhisattva and mahasattva named Great Joy of Preaching, who understood the doubts that were in the minds of the heavenly and human beings, asuras and other beings of all the world. He said to the Buddha: "World-Honored One, for what reason has this treasure tower risen up out of the earth? And why does this voice issue from its midst?"

At that time the Buddha said: "Bodhisattva Great Joy of Preaching, in the treasure tower is the complete body of a Thus Come One. Long ago, an immeasurable thousand, ten thousand, million asamkhyas of worlds to the east, in a land called Treasure Purity, there was a Buddha named Many Treasures. When this Buddha was originally carrying out the bodhisattva way, he made a great vow, saying, 'If, after I have become a Buddha and entered extinction, in the lands in the ten directions there is any place where the Lotus Sutra is preached, then my funerary tower, in order that I may listen to the sutra, will come forth and appear in that spot to testify to the sutra and praise its excellence.'

"When that Buddha had finished carrying out the Buddha way and was on the point of passing into extinction, in the midst of the great assembly of heavenly and human beings he said to the monks, 'After I have passed into extinction, if there are those who wish to offer alms to my complete body, then they should erect a great tower.' That Buddha, through his transcendental powers and the power of his vow, insures that, throughout the worlds in the ten directions, no matter in what place, if there are those who preach the Lotus Sutra, this treasure tower will in all cases come forth and appear in their presence, and his complete body will be in the tower, speaking words of praise and saying, Excellent, excellent!

"Great Joy of Preaching, now this tower of the Thus Come One Many Treasures, because it heard the preaching of the Lotus Sutra, has come forth out of the ground and speaks words of praise, saying, Excellent, excellent!"

At this time Bodhisattva Great Joy of Preaching, knowing the supernatural powers of the Thus Come One, spoke to the Buddha, saying, "World-Honored One, we wish to see the body of this Buddha."

The Buddha said to the bodhisattva and mahasattva Great Joy of Preaching, "This Many Treasures Buddha has taken a profound vow, saying, 'When my treasure tower, in order to listen to the Lotus Sutra, comes forth into the presence of one of the Buddhas, if there should be those who wish me to show my body to the four kinds of believers, then let the various Buddhas who are emanations of that Buddha and who are preaching the Law in the worlds in the ten directions all return and gather around that Buddha in a single spot. Only when that has been done will my body become visible.' Great Joy of Preaching, I will now gather together the various Buddhas that are emanations of my body and that are preaching the Law in the worlds in the ten directions."

Great Joy of Preaching said to the Buddha, "World-Honored One, I and the others also wish to see these Buddhas that are emanations of the World-Honored One, and to make obeisance to them and offer alms."

At that time the Buddha emitted a ray of light from the tuft of white hair [between his eyebrows], immediately making visible the Buddhas in the eastern region in lands as numerous as five hundred ten thousand million nayutas of Ganges sands. The earth in all these lands was made of crystal, and the lands were adorned with jeweled trees and jeweled robes. Countless thousands, ten thousands, millions of bodhisattvas filled them, and everywhere were hung jeweled curtains, with jeweled nets covering them over. The Buddhas in these lands preached the various doctrines of the Law with great and wonderful voices, and one could see immeasurable thousands, ten thousands, millions of bodhisattvas filling all these lands and preaching the Law for the assembly. In the southern, western and northern regions as well, and in the four intermediate quarters and up and down, wherever the beam from the tuft of white hair, a characteristic feature of the Buddha, shone, the same was true.

At that time the Buddhas of the ten directions each spoke to his multitude of bodhisattvas, saying, "Good men, now I must go to the saha world, to the place where Shakyamuni Buddha is, and also offer alms to the treasure tower of Many Treasures Thus Come One."

The saha world thereupon immediately changed into a place of cleanness and purity. The ground was made of lapis lazuli, jeweled trees adorned it, and ropes of gold marked off the eight highways. There were no villages, towns or cities, great seas or rivers, mountains, streams or forests; great jeweled incense was burning there and mandarava flowers covered the ground all over. Jeweled nets and curtains were spread above, hung with jeweled bells, and the members of this assembly alone were gathered there, all other heavenly and human beings having been moved to another region.

At that time the Buddhas, each with a great bodhisattva to act as his attendant, arrived in the saha world and proceeded to a position beneath one of the jeweled trees. Each of these jeweled trees was five hundred yojanas high and adorned with branches, leaves, flowers and fruit in due proportion. Under all the jeweled trees were lion seats five yojanas in height, and these too were decorated with large jewels. At that time each of the Buddhas took one of these seats, seating himself in cross-legged position. In this way the seats were filled throughout the thousand-millionfold world, but still there was no end even to the emanations of Shakyamuni Buddha arriving from merely one direction.

At that time Shakyamuni Buddha, wishing to provide space for all the Buddhas that were emanations of his body, in addition transformed two hundred ten thousand million nayutas of lands in each of the eight directions, making them all clean and pure and without hells, hungry spirits, beasts or asuras. He also moved all their heavenly and human beings to another region. The ground in these lands that he had transformed was also made of lapis lazuli. Jeweled trees adorned them, each tree five hundred yojanas high and adorned with branches, leaves, flowers and fruit in due proportion. There were jeweled lion seats under all the trees, five yojanas in height and ornamented with various kinds of treasures. These lands too were without great seas or rivers, or any kingly ranges of mountains such as the Muchilinda Mountains, Mahamuchilinda Mountains, Iron Encircling Mountains, Great Iron Encircling Mountains, or Mount Sumeru. The whole area comprised a single Buddha land, a jeweled region level and smooth. Curtains crisscrossed with festoons of jewels were spread everywhere, banners and canopies hung down, great jeweled incense burned, and heavenly jeweled flowers covered the ground all around.

Shakyamuni Buddha, in order to provide seats for all the Buddhas that were arriving, once more transformed two hundred ten thousand million nayutas of lands in each of the eight directions, making them all clean and pure and without hells, hungry spirits, beasts or asuras. He also moved all the heavenly and human beings to another region. The ground in these lands that he had transformed was likewise made of lapis lazuli. Jeweled trees adorned the lands, each tree five hundred yojanas in height and adorned with branches, leaves, flowers and fruit in due proportion. There were jeweled lion seats under all the trees, five yojanas in height and ornamented with great jewels. These lands too were without great seas or rivers, or any kingly ranges such as the Muchilinda Mountains, Mahamuchilinda Mountains, Iron Encircling Mountains, Great Iron Encircling Mountains, or Mount Sumeru, the whole area comprising a single Buddha land, a jeweled region level and smooth. Curtains crisscrossed with festoons of jewels were spread everywhere, banners and canopies hung down, great jeweled incense burned, and heavenly jeweled flowers covered the ground all around.

At that time the emanations of Shakyamuni Buddha from the eastern region, Buddhas in lands equal in number to hundreds, thousands, ten thousands, millions of nayutas of Ganges sands, each preaching the Law, had assembled there. And bit by bit the Buddhas from the ten directions all came and assembled in this way and were seated in the eight directions. At this time each of the directions was filled with Buddhas, Thus Come Ones, in four hundred ten thousand million nayutas of lands.

At this time the Buddhas, each seated on a lion seat under one of the jeweled trees, all dispatched their attendants to go and greet Shakyamuni Buddha. Each Buddha presented his attendant with a handful of jeweled flowers and said, "Good man, you must go to Mount Gridhrakuta to the place where Shakyamuni Buddha is and speak to him as I instruct you. Say, 'Are your illnesses few, are your worries few? In spirit and vigor are you well and happy? And are the bodhisattvas and voice-hearers all well and at peace?' Then take these jeweled flowers and scatter them over the Buddha as an offering, and say, 'The Buddha So-and-so would like to participate in the opening of this treasure tower.'

All the Buddhas dispatched their attendants to speak in this manner. At that time Shakyamuni Buddha saw the Buddhas that were his emanations all assembled, each sitting on a lion seat, and heard all these Buddhas say that they wished to participate in the opening of the treasure tower. Immediately he rose from his seat and stationed himself in midair. All the four kinds of believers likewise stood up, pressed their palms together and gazed at the Buddha with a single mind.

Shakyamuni Buddha with the fingers of his right hand then opened the door of the tower of seven treasures. A loud sound issued from it, like the sound of a lock and crossbar being removed from a great city gate, and at once all the members of the assembly caught sight of Many Treasures Thus Come One seated on a lion seat inside the treasure tower, his body whole and unimpaired, sitting as though engaged in meditation. And they heard him say, "Excellent, excellent, Shakyamuni Buddha! You have preached this Lotus Sutra in a spirited manner. I have come here in order that I may hear this sutra."

At that time the four kinds of believers, observing this Buddha who had passed into extinction immeasurable thousands, ten thousands, millions of kalpas in the past speaking in this way, marveled at what they had never known before and took the masses of heavenly jeweled flowers and scattered them over Many Treasures Buddha and Shakyamuni Buddha.

At that time Many Treasures Buddha offered half of his seat in the treasure tower to Shakyamuni Buddha, saying, "Shakyamuni Buddha, sit here!" Shakyamuni Buddha at once entered the tower and took half of the seat, seating himself in cross-legged position.

At that time the members of the great assembly, seeing the two Thus Come Ones seated cross-legged on the lion seat in the tower of seven treasures, all thought to themselves, These Buddhas are seated high up and far away! If only the Thus Come Ones would employ their transcendental powers to enable all of us to join them there in the air!

Immediately Shakyamuni Buddha used his transcendental powers to lift all the members of the great assembly up into the air. And in a loud voice he addressed all the four kinds of believers, saying, "Who is capable of broadly preaching the Lotus Sutra of the Wonderful Law in this saha world? Now is the time to do so, for before long the Thus Come One will enter nirvana. The Buddha wishes to entrust this Lotus Sutra of the Wonderful Law to someone so that it may be preserved."

At that time the World-Honored One, wishing to state his meaning once more, spoke in verse form, saying:

> This holy lord, this World-Honored One,
> though he passed into extinction long ago,
> still seats himself in the treasure tower,
> coming here for the sake of the Law.
> You people, why then do you not also
> strive for the sake of the Law?
> This Buddha passed into extinction
> an endless number of kalpas ago,
> but in many places he comes to listen to the Law
> because such opportunities are hard to encounter.
> This Buddha originally made a vow, saying,
> "After I have passed into extinction,
> wherever I may go, in whatever place,
> my constant aim will be to hear the Law!"
> In addition, these emanations of my body,
> Buddhas in immeasurable numbers
> like Ganges sands,
> have come, desiring to hear the Law,
> and so they may see Many Treasures Thus Come One
> who has passed into extinction.

Each has abandoned his wonderful land,
as well as his host of disciples,
the heavenly and human beings, dragons and spirits,
and all the offerings they give him,
and has come to this place on purpose
to make certain the Law will long endure.
In order to seat these Buddhas
I have employed transcendental powers,
moving immeasurable multitudes,
causing lands to be clean and pure,
leading each of these Buddhas
to the foot of a jeweled tree,
adorned as lotus blossoms
adorn a clear cool pond.
Beneath these jeweled trees
are lion seats,
and the Buddhas seat themselves on them,
adorning them with their brilliance
like a huge torch burning
in the darkness of the night.
A wonderful incense exudes from their bodies,
pervading the lands in the ten directions.
Living beings are wrapped in the aroma,
unable to restrain their joy,
as though a great wind
were tossing the branches of small trees.
Through this expedient means
they make certain that the Law will long endure.
So I say to the great assembly:
After I have passed into extinction,
who can guard and uphold,
read and recite this sutra?
Now in the presence of the Buddha
let him come forward and speak his vow!
This Many Treasures Buddha,
though he passed into extinction long ago,
because of his great vow
roars the lion's roar.

Many Treasures Thus Come One, I myself,
and these emanation Buddhas who have gathered here,
surely know this is our aim.
You sons of the Buddha,
who can guard the Law?
Let him make a great vow
to ensure that it will long endure!
He who is capable of guarding
the Law of this sutra
will thereby have offered alms
to me and to Many Treasures.
This Many Treasures Buddha
dwelling in his treasure tower
journeys constantly throughout the ten directions
for the sake of this sutra.
One who guards this sutra will also have offered alms
to the emanation Buddhas who have come here
adorning and making brilliant
all the various worlds.
If one preaches this sutra,
he will be able to see me
and Many Treasures Thus Come One
and these emanation Buddhas.
All you good men,
each of you must consider carefully!
This is a difficult matter—
it is proper you should make a great vow.
The other sutras
number as many as Ganges sands,
but though you expound those sutras,
that is not worth regarding as difficult.
If you were to seize Mount Sumeru
and fling it far off
to the measureless Buddha lands,
that too would not be difficult.
If you used the toe of your foot
to move the thousand-millionfold world,
booting it far away to other lands,

that too would not be difficult.
If you stood in the Summit of Being heaven
and for the sake of the assembly
preached countless other sutras,
that too would not be difficult.
But if after the Buddha has entered extinction,
in the time of evil,
you can preach this sutra,
that will be difficult indeed!
If there were a person
who took the empty sky in his hand
and walked all around with it,
that would not be difficult.
But if after I have passed into extinction
one can write out and embrace this sutra
and cause others to write it out,
that will be difficult indeed!
If one took the great earth,
placed it on his toenail,
and ascended with it to the Brahma heaven,
that would not be difficult.
But if after the Buddha has passed into extinction,
in the time of evil,
one can even for a little while read this sutra,
that will be difficult indeed!
If, when the fires come at the end of the kalpa,
one can load dry grass on his back
and enter the fire without being burned,
that would not be difficult.
But after I have passed into extinction
if one can embrace this sutra
and expound it to even one person,
that will be difficult indeed!
If one were to embrace this storehouse
of eighty-four thousand doctrines,
the twelve divisions of the sutras,
and expound it to others,
causing listeners

to acquire the six transcendental powers—
though one could do that,
that would not be difficult.
But after I have entered extinction
if one can listen to and accept this sutra
and ask about its meaning,
that will be difficult indeed!
If a person expounds the Law,
allowing thousands, ten thousands, millions,
immeasurable numbers of living beings
equal to Ganges sands
to become arhats
endowed with the six transcendental powers,
though one might confer such benefits,
that would not be difficult.
But after I have entered extinction
if one can honor and embrace
a sutra such as this one,
that will be difficult indeed!
For the sake of the Buddha way
in immeasurable numbers of lands
from the beginning until now
I have widely preached many sutras,
and among them
this sutra is foremost.
If one can uphold this,
he will be upholding the Buddha's body.
All you good men,
after I have entered extinction
who can accept and uphold,
read and recite this sutra?
Now in the presence of the Buddha
let him come forward and speak his vow!
This sutra is hard to uphold;
if one can uphold it even for a short while
I will surely rejoice
and so will the other Buddhas.
A person who can do this

wins the admiration of the Buddhas.
This is what is meant by valor,
this is what is meant by diligence.
This is what is called observing the precepts
and practicing dhuta.
This way one will quickly attain
the unsurpassed Buddha way.
And if in future existences
one can read and uphold this sutra,
he will be a true son of the Buddha,
dwelling in a land spotless and good.
If after the Buddha has passed into extinction
one can understand the meaning of this sutra,
he will be the eyes of the world
for heavenly and human beings.
If in that fearful age
one can preach this sutra for even a moment,
he will deserve to receive alms
from all heavenly and human beings.

12

DEVADATTA

At that time the Buddha addressed the bodhisattvas, the heavenly and human beings, and the four kinds of believers, saying: "Immeasurable kalpas in the past, I sought the Lotus Sutra without ever flagging. During those many kalpas, I constantly appeared as the ruler of a kingdom who made a vow to seek the unsurpassed bodhi. His mind never wavered or turned aside, and in his desire to fulfill the six paramitas he diligently distributed alms, never stinting in heart, whether the gift was elephants or horses, the seven rare articles, countries, cities, wife, children, maidservants, menservants, or his own head, eyes, marrow and brain, his own flesh and limbs. He did not begrudge even his own being and life. At that period the human life span was immeasurably long. But for the sake of the Law this king abandoned his kingdom and throne, delegated the government to the crown prince, sounded drums and sent out proclamations, seeking the Law in four directions and saying, 'Who can expound the Great Vehicle for me? To the end of my life I will be his provider and servant!'

"At that time there was a seer who came to the king and said, 'I have a Great Vehicle text called the Sutra of the Lotus of the Wonderful Law. If you will never disobey me, I will expound it for you.'

"When the king heard these words of the seer, he danced for joy. At once he accompanied the seer, providing him with whatever he needed, picking fruit, drawing water, gathering firewood, setting out meals, even offering his own body as a couch and seat, never stinting in body or mind. He served the seer in this manner for a thousand years, all for the sake of the Law, working diligently, acting as a provider and seeing to it that the seer lacked for nothing."

At that time the World-Honored One, wishing to state his meaning once more, spoke in verse form, saying:

> I recall those departed kalpas of the past
> when in order to seek the great Law,
> though I was the ruler of a worldly kingdom,
> I was not greedy to satisfy the five desires
> but instead struck the bell, crying in four quarters,
> "Who possesses the great Law?
> If he will explain and preach it for me
> I will be his slave and servant!"
> At that time there was a seer named Asita
> who came and announced to this great king,
> "I have a subtle and wonderful Law,
> rarely known in this world.
> If you will undertake religious practice
> I will expound it for you."
> When the king heard the seer's words
> his heart was filled with great joy.
> Immediately he accompanied the seer,
> providing him with whatever he needed,

gathering firewood, fruit and wild rice,
presenting them at appropriate times with respect and
    reverence.
Because the wonderful Law was in his thoughts
he never flagged in body or mind.
For the sake of living beings everywhere
he diligently sought the great Law,
taking no heed for himself
or for the gratification of the five desires.
Therefore the ruler of a great kingdom
through diligent seeking was able to acquire this Law
and eventually to attain Buddhahood,
as I will now explain to you.

The Buddha said to the monks: "The king at that time was I myself,
and the seer was the man who is now Devadatta. All because Devadatta
was a good friend to me, I was able to become fully endowed with the
six paramitas, with pity, compassion, joy, and indifference, with the
thirty-two features, the eighty characteristics, the purple-tinged
golden color, the ten powers, the four kinds of fearlessness, the four
methods of winning people, the eighteen unshared properties, and the
transcendental powers and the power of the way. The fact that I have
attained impartial and correct enlightenment and can save living beings
on a broad scale is all due to Devadatta, who was a good friend."

Then the Buddha said to the four kinds of believers: "Devadatta,
after immeasurable kalpas have passed, will attain Buddhahood. He
will be called Heavenly King Thus Come One, worthy of offerings, of
right and universal knowledge, perfect clarity and conduct, well gone,
understanding the world, unexcelled worthy, trainer of people, teacher
of heavenly and human beings, Buddha, World-Honored One. His
world will be called Heavenly Way, and at that time Heavenly King
Buddha will abide in the world for twenty medium kalpas, broadly
preaching the wonderful Law for the sake of living beings. Living
beings numerous as Ganges sands will attain the fruit of arhatship.
Immeasurable numbers of living beings will conceive the desire to
become pratyekabuddhas, living beings numerous as Ganges sands will
conceive a desire for the unsurpassed way, will gain the truth of
birthlessness, and will never regress. After Heavenly King Buddha

enters parinirvana, his Correct Law will endure in the world for twenty medium kalpas. The relics from his whole body will be housed in a tower built of the seven treasures, sixty yojanas in height and forty yojanas in width and depth. All the heavenly and human beings will take assorted flowers, powdered incense, incense for burning, paste incense, clothing, necklaces, streamers and banners, jeweled canopies, music and songs of praise and offer them with obeisance to the wonderful seven-jeweled tower. Immeasurable numbers of living beings will attain the fruits of arhatship, numberless living beings will become enlightened as pratyekabuddhas, and unimaginable numbers of living beings will conceive a desire for bodhi and will reach the level of no regression."

The Buddha said to the monks: "In future ages if there are good men or good women who, on hearing the Devadatta chapter of the Lotus Sutra of the Wonderful Law, believe and revere it with pure hearts and harbor no doubts or perplexities, they will never fall into hell or the realm of hungry spirits or of beasts, but will be born in the presence of the Buddhas of the ten directions, and in the place where they are born they will constantly hear this sutra. If they are born among human or heavenly beings, they will enjoy exceedingly wonderful delights, and if they are born in the presence of a Buddha, they will be born by transformation from lotus flowers."

At that time there was a bodhisattva who was among the followers of Many Treasures World-Honored One from the lower region and whose name was Wisdom Accumulated. He said to Many Treasures Buddha, "Shall we return to our homeland?"

Shakyamuni Buddha said to Wisdom Accumulated, "Good man, wait a little while. There is a bodhisattva named Manjushri here whom you should see. Debate and discuss the wonderful Law with him, and then you may return to your homeland."

At that time Manjushri was seated on a thousand-petaled lotus blossom big as a carriage wheel, and the bodhisattvas who had come with him were also seated on jeweled lotus blossoms. Manjushri had emerged in a natural manner from the palace of the dragon king Sagara in the great ocean and was suspended in the air. Proceeding to Holy Eagle Peak, he descended from the lotus blossom and, having entered the presence of the Buddhas, bowed his head and paid obeisance to the feet of the two World-Honored Ones. When he had concluded these gestures of respect, he went to where Wisdom Accumulated was and exchanged greetings with him, and then retired and sat at one side.

Bodhisattva Wisdom Accumulated questioned Manjushri, saying, "When you went to the palace of the dragon king, how many living beings did you convert?"

Manjushri replied, "The number is immeasurable, incapable of calculation. The mouth cannot express it, the mind cannot fathom it. Wait a moment and there will be proof."

Before he had finished speaking, countless bodhisattvas seated on jeweled lotus blossoms emerged from the ocean and proceeded to Holy Eagle Peak, where they remained suspended in the air. These bodhisattvas had all been converted and saved by Manjushri. They had carried out all the bodhisattva practices and all discussed and expounded the six paramitas with one another. Those who had originally been voice-hearers expounded the practices of the voice-hearer when they were in the air, but now all were practicing the Great Vehicle principle of emptiness.

Manjushri said to Wisdom Accumulated, "The work of teaching and converting carried out in the ocean was as you can see."

At that time Bodhisattva Wisdom Accumulated recited these verses of praise:

> Of great wisdom and virtue, brave and stalwart,
> you have converted and saved immeasurable beings.
> Now those in this great assembly,
> as well as I myself, have all seen them.
> You expound the principle of the true entity,
> open up the Law of the single vehicle,
> broadly guiding the many beings,
> causing them quickly to attain bodhi.

Manjushri said, "When I was in the ocean I constantly expounded the Lotus Sutra of the Wonderful Law alone."

Bodhisattva Wisdom Accumulated questioned Manjushri, saying, "This sutra is very profound, subtle and wonderful, a treasure among sutras, a rarity in the world. Are there perhaps any living beings who, by earnestly and diligently practicing this sutra, have been able to attain Buddhahood quickly?"

Manjushri replied, "There is the daughter of the dragon king Sagara, who has just turned eight. Her wisdom has keen roots and she is good at understanding the root activities and deeds of living beings. She has mastered the dharanis, has been able to accept and embrace all the storehouse of profound secrets preached by the Buddhas, has entered deep into meditation, thoroughly grasped the doctrines, and in the space of an instant conceived the desire for bodhi and reached the level of no regression. Her eloquence knows no hindrance, and she thinks of living beings with compassion as though they were her own children. She is fully endowed with blessings, and when it comes to conceiving in mind and expounding by mouth, she is subtle, wonderful, comprehensive and great. Kind, compassionate, benevolent, yielding, she is gentle and refined in will, capable of attaining bodhi."

Bodhisattva Wisdom Accumulated said, "When I observe Shakyamuni Thus Come One, I see that for immeasurable kalpas he carried out harsh and difficult practices, accumulating merit, piling up virtue, seeking the way of the bodhisattva without ever resting. I observe that throughout the thousand-millionfold world, there is not a single spot tiny as a mustard seed where this bodhisattva failed to sacrifice body and life for the sake of living beings. Only after he had done that was he able to complete the bodhi way. I cannot believe that this girl in the space of an instant could actually achieve correct enlightenment."

Before his words had come to an end, the dragon king's daughter suddenly appeared before the Buddha, bowed her head in obeisance, and then retired to one side, reciting these verses of praise:

He profoundly understands the signs of guilt and good fortune
and illuminates the ten directions everywhere.
His subtle, wonderful pure Dharma body
is endowed with the thirty-two features;
the eighty characteristics
adorn his Dharma body.
Heavenly and human beings gaze up in awe,
dragons and spirits all pay honor and respect;
among all living beings,

none who do not hold him in reverence.
And having heard his teachings, I have attained bodhi—
the Buddha alone can bear witness to this.
I unfold the doctrines of the Great Vehicle
to rescue living beings from suffering.

At that time Shariputra said to the dragon girl, "You suppose that in this short time you have been able to attain the unsurpassed way. But this is difficult to believe. Why? Because a woman's body is soiled and defiled, not a vessel for the Law. How could you attain the unsurpassed bodhi? The road to Buddhahood is long and far-stretching. Only after one has spent immeasurable kalpas pursuing austerities, accumulating deeds, practicing all kinds of paramitas, can one finally achieve success. Moreover, a woman is subject to the five obstacles. First, she cannot become a Brahma heavenly king. Second, she cannot become the king Shakra. Third, she cannot become a devil king. Fourth, she cannot become a wheel-turning sage king. Fifth, she cannot become a Buddha. How then could a woman like you be able to attain Buddhahood so quickly?"

At that time the dragon girl had a precious jewel worth as much as the thousand-millionfold world which she presented to the Buddha. The Buddha immediately accepted it. The dragon girl said to Bodhisattva Wisdom Accumulated and to the venerable one, Shariputra, "I presented the precious jewel and the World-Honored One accepted it— was that not quickly done?"

They replied, "Very quickly!"

The girl said, "Employ your supernatural powers and watch me attain Buddhahood. It will be even quicker than that!"

At that time the members of the assembly all saw the dragon girl in the space of an instant change into a man and carry out all the practices of a bodhisattva, immediately proceeding to the Spotless World of the south, taking a seat on a jeweled lotus, and attaining impartial and correct enlightenment. With the thirty-two features and the eighty characteristics, he expounded the wonderful Law for all living beings everywhere in the ten directions.

At that time in the saha world the bodhisattvas, voice-hearers, gods, dragons and others of the eight kinds of guardians, human and non-human beings all from a distance saw the dragon girl become a Buddha and preach the Law to all the human and heavenly beings in the assembly at that time. Their hearts were filled with great joy and all from a distance paid reverent obeisance. Immeasurable living beings, hearing the Law, understood it and were able to reach the level of no regression. Immeasurable living beings received prophecies that they would gain the way. The Spotless World quaked and trembled in six different ways. Three thousand living beings of the saha world remained on the level of no regression. Three thousand living beings conceived a desire for bodhi and received prophecies of enlightenment. Bodhisattva Wisdom Accumulated, Shariputra and all the other members of the assembly silently believed and accepted these things.

15

EMERGING FROM
THE EARTH

At that time the bodhisattvas and mahasattvas who had gathered from the lands of the other directions, greater in number than the sands of eight Ganges, stood up in the midst of the great assembly, pressed their palms together, bowed in obeisance and said to the Buddha: "World-Honored One, if you will permit us in the age after the Buddha has entered extinction to diligently and earnestly protect, read, recite, copy and offer alms to this sutra in the saha world, we will preach it widely throughout this land!"

At that time the Buddha said to the bodhisattvas and mahasattvas: "Leave off, good men! There is no need for you to protect this sutra. Why? Because in this saha world of mine there are bodhisattvas and mahasattvas who are as numerous as the sands of sixty thousand Ganges, and each of these bodhisattvas has a retinue equal to the sands of sixty thousand Ganges. After I have entered extinction these persons will be able to protect, read, recite and widely preach this sutra."

When the Buddha spoke these words, the earth of the thousand-millionfold countries of the saha world all trembled and split open, and out of it emerged at the same instant immeasurable thousands, ten thousands, millions of bodhisattvas and mahasattvas. The bodies of these bodhisattvas were all golden in hue, with the thirty-two features and an immeasurable brightness. Previously they had all been dwelling in the world of empty space underneath the saha world. But when these bodhisattvas heard the voice of Shakyamuni Buddha speaking, they came up from below.

Each one of these bodhisattvas was the leader of his own great assembly, and each brought with him a retinue equal in number to the sands of sixty thousand Ganges. To say nothing of those who brought retinues equal to the sands of fifty thousand, forty thousand, thirty thousand, twenty thousand, or ten thousand Ganges. Or a retinue equal to as little as the sands of one Ganges, half a Ganges, one fourth of a Ganges, or as little as one part in a thousand, ten thousand, a million nayutas of Ganges. Or those whose retinue was only one thousand ten thousand million nayutas. Or only a million ten thousand. Or only a thousand ten thousand, a hundred ten thousand, or just ten thousand. Or only one thousand, one hundred, or ten. Or who brought with them only five, four, three, two or one disciple. Or those who came alone, preferring to carry out solitary practices. Such were they, then, immeasurable, boundless, beyond anything that can be known through calculation, simile or parable.

After these bodhisattvas had emerged from the earth, they each one proceeded to the wonderful tower of seven treasures suspended in the sky where Many Treasures Thus Come One and Shakyamuni Buddha were. On reaching it, they turned to the two World-Honored Ones, bowed their heads and made obeisance at their feet. They also all performed obeisance to the Buddhas seated on lion seats underneath the jeweled trees. Then they circled around to the right three times, pressed their palms together in a gesture of respect, utilizing the bodhisattvas' various methods of praising to deliver praises, and then took up a position to one side, gazing up in joy at the two World-

Honored Ones. While these bodhisattvas and mahasattvas who had emerged from the earth were employing the bodhisattvas' various methods of praising to praise the Buddhas, an interval of fifty small kalpas passed by.

At that time Shakyamuni Buddha sat silent, and the four kinds of believers likewise all remained silent for fifty small kalpas, but because of the supernatural powers of the Buddha, it was made to seem to the members of the great assembly like only half a day.

At that time the four kinds of believers, also because of the supernatural powers of the Buddha, saw these bodhisattvas filling the sky over immeasurable hundreds, thousands, ten thousands, and millions of lands. Among these bodhisattvas were four leaders. The first was called Superior Practices, the second was called Boundless Practices, the third was called Pure Practices, and the fourth was called Firmly Established Practices. These four bodhisattvas were the foremost leaders and guiding teachers among all the group. In the presence of the great assembly, each one of these pressed his palms together, gazed at Shakyamuni Buddha, and inquired: "World-Honored One, are your illnesses few, are your worries few, are your practices proceeding comfortably? Do those whom you propose to save readily receive instruction? Does the effort not cause the World-Honored One to become weary and spent?"

At that time the four great bodhisattvas spoke in verse form, saying:

> Is the World-Honored One comfortable,
> with few illnesses, few worries?
> In teaching and converting living beings,
> can you do so without fatigue and weariness?
> And do living beings
> receive instruction readily or not?
> Does it not cause the World-Honored One
> to become weary and spent?

At that time in the midst of the great assembly of bodhisattvas the World-Honored One spoke these words: "Just so, just so, good men! The Thus Come One is well and happy, with few ills and few worries.

The living beings are readily converted and saved and I am not weary or spent. Why? Because for age after age in the past the living beings have constantly received my instruction. And also they have offered alms and paid reverence to the Buddhas of the past and have planted various good roots. So when these living beings see me for the first time and listen to my preaching, they all immediately believe and accept it, entering into the wisdom of the Thus Come One, with the exception of those who earlier practiced and studied the Lesser Vehicle. And now I will make it possible for these persons to listen to this sutra and enter the wisdom of the Buddha."

At that time the [four] great bodhisattvas spoke in verse form, saying:

> Excellent, excellent,
> great hero, World-Honored One!
> The living beings
> are readily converted and saved.
> They know how to inquire about
> the most profound wisdom of the Buddha,
> and having heard, they believe and understand it.
> We are accordingly overjoyed.

At that time the World-Honored One praised the great bodhisattvas who led the group, saying: "Excellent, excellent, good men! You know how to rejoice in your hearts for the Thus Come One."

At that time the bodhisattva Maitreya and the multitude of bodhisattvas equal in number to the sands of eight thousand Ganges all thought to themselves: Never in the past have we seen or heard of such a great multitude of bodhisattvas and mahasattvas as these who have emerged from the earth and now stand before the World-Honored One pressing their palms together, offering alms, and inquiring about the Thus Come One!

At that time the bodhisattva and mahasattva Maitreya, knowing the thought that was in the minds of the bodhisattvas as numerous as the sands of eight thousand Ganges, and wishing also to resolve his own doubts, pressed his palms together, turned to the Buddha and made this inquiry in verse form:

Immeasurable thousands, ten thousands, millions,
a great host of bodhisattvas
such as was never seen in the past—
I beg the most honored of two-legged beings to explain
where they have come from,
what causes and conditions bring them together!
Huge in body, with great transcendental powers,
unfathomable in wisdom,
firm in their intent and thought,
with the power of great perseverance,
the kind living beings delight to see—
where have they come from?
Each one of these bodhisattvas
brings with him a retinue
immeasurable in number
like the sands of the Ganges.
Some of these great bodhisattvas
bring numbers equal to sixty thousand Ganges sands.
And this great multitude
with a single mind seek the Buddha way.
These great teachers
equal in number to sixty thousand Ganges sands
together come to offer alms to the Buddha
and to guard and uphold this sutra.
More numerous are those with followers
like the sands of fifty thousand Ganges,
those with followers like the sands of forty thousand,
    thirty thousand,
twenty thousand, ten thousand,
one thousand, one hundred,
or the sands of a single Ganges,
half a Ganges, one third, one fourth,
or only one part in a million ten thousand;
those with one thousand, ten thousand nayutas,
ten thousand, a million disciples,
or half a million—
they are more numerous still.
Those with a million or ten thousand followers,

a thousand or a hundred,
fifty or ten,
three, two, or one,
or those who come alone without followers,
delighting in solitude,
all coming to where the Buddha is—
they are even more numerous than those described above.
If one should try to use an abacus
to calculate the number of this great multitude,
though he spent as many kalpas as Ganges sands
he could never know the full sum.
This host of bodhisattvas
with their great dignity, virtue and diligence—
who preached the Law for them,
who taught and converted them and brought them to this?
Under whom did they first set their minds on enlightenment,
what Buddha's Law do they praise and proclaim?
What sutra do they embrace and carry out,
what Buddha way do they practice?
These bodhisattvas
possess transcendental powers and the power of great wisdom.
The earth in four directions trembles and splits
and they all emerge from out of it.
World-Honored One, from times past
I have seen nothing like this!
I beg you to tell me where they come from,
the name of the land.
I have constantly journeyed from land to land
but never have I seen such a thing!
In this whole multitude
there is not one person that I know.
Suddenly they have come up from the earth—
I beg you to explain the cause.
The members of this great assembly now,
the immeasurable hundreds, thousands, millions
of bodhisattvas,
all want to know these things.
Regarding the causes that govern the beginning and end

of this multitude of bodhisattvas,
possessor of immeasurable virtue, World-Honored One,
we beg you to dispel the doubts of the assembly!

At that time the Buddhas who were emanations of Shakyamuni Buddha and had arrived from immeasurable thousands, ten thousands, millions of lands in other directions, were seated cross-legged on lion seats under the jeweled trees in the eight directions. The attendants of these Buddhas all saw the great multitude of bodhisattvas who had emerged from the earth in the four directions of the thousand-millionfold world and were suspended in the air, and each one said to his respective Buddha: "World-Honored One, this great multitude of immeasurable, boundless asamkhyas of bodhisattvas—where did they come from?"

At that time each of the Buddhas spoke to his attendants, saying: "Good men, wait a moment. There is a bodhisattva and mahasattva named Maitreya who has received a prophecy from Shakyamuni Buddha that he will be the next hereafter to become a Buddha. He has already inquired about this matter and the Buddha is now about to answer him. You should take this opportunity to listen to what he says."

At that time Shakyamuni Buddha said to the bodhisattva Maitreya: "Excellent, excellent, Ajita, that you should question the Buddha about this great affair. All of you with a single mind should don the armor of diligence and determine to be firm in intent. The Thus Come One wishes now to summon forth and declare the wisdom of the Buddhas, the freely exercised transcendental power of the Buddhas, the power of the Buddhas that has the lion's ferocity, the fierce and greatly forceful power of the Buddhas."

At that time the World-Honored One, wishing to state his meaning once more, spoke in verse form, saying:

> Be diligent and of a single mind,
> for I wish to explain this affair.
> Have no doubts or regrets—
> the Buddha wisdom is hard to fathom.
> Now you must put forth the power of faith,
> abiding in patience and goodness.

A Law which in the past was never heard
you will now all be able to hear.
Now I will bring you ease and consolation—
do not harbor doubts or fears.
The Buddha has nothing but truthful words,
his wisdom cannot be measured.
This foremost Law that he has gained
is very profound, incapable of analysis.
He will now expound it—
you must listen with a single mind.

At that time the World-Honored One, having spoken these verses, said to the bodhisattva Maitreya: "With regard to this great multitude I now say this to you. Ajita, these bodhisattvas and mahasattvas who in immeasurable and countless asamkhyas have emerged from the earth and whom you have never seen before in the past—when I had attained anuttara-samyak-sambodhi in this saha world, I converted and guided these bodhisattvas, trained their minds and caused them to develop a longing for the way. These bodhisattvas have all been dwelling in the world of empty space underneath the saha world. They read, recite, understand the various scriptures, ponder them, make distinctions and keep them correctly in mind.

"Ajita, these good men take no delight in being in the assembly and indulging in much talk. Their delight is constantly to be in a quiet place, exerting themselves diligently and never resting. Nor do they linger among human or heavenly beings, but constantly delight in profound wisdom, being free from all hindrances. And they constantly delight in the Law of the Buddhas, diligently and with a single mind pursuing unsurpassed wisdom."

At that time the World-Honored One, wishing to state his meaning once more, spoke in verse form, saying:

Ajita, you should understand this.
These great bodhisattvas
for countless kalpas
have practiced the Buddha wisdom.
All have been converted by me;
I caused them to set their minds on the great way.

These are my sons,
they dwell in this world,
constantly carrying out dhuta practices,
preferring a quiet place,
rejecting the fret and confusion of the great assembly,
taking no delight in much talk.
In this manner these sons
study and practice my way and Law.
And in order that day and night with constant diligence
they may seek the Buddha way,
in this saha world
they dwell in the empty space in its lower part.
Firm in the power of will and concentration,
with constant diligence seeking wisdom,
they expound various wonderful doctrines
and their minds are without fear.
When I was in the city of Gaya,
seated beneath the bodhi tree,
I attained the highest, the correct enlightenment
and turned the wheel of the unsurpassed Law.
Thereafter I taught and converted them,
caused them for the first time to set their minds on the way.
Now all of them dwell in the stage of no regression,
and all in time will be able to become Buddhas.
What I speak now are true words—
with a single mind you must believe them!
Ever since the long distant past
I have been teaching and converting this multitude.

At that time the bodhisattva and mahasattva Maitreya, as well as the countless other bodhisattvas, found doubts and perplexities rising in their minds. They were puzzled at this thing that had never happened before and thought to themselves: How could the World-Honored One in such a short space of time have taught and converted an immeasurable, boundless asamkhya number of great bodhisattvas of this sort and enabled them to dwell in anuttara-samyak-sambodhi?

Thereupon Maitreya said to the Buddha: "World-Honored One, when the Thus Come One was crown prince, you left the palace of the

Shakyas and sat in the place of practice not far from the city of Gaya, and there attained anuttara-samyak-sambodhi. Barely forty years or more have passed since then. World-Honored One, how in that short time could you have accomplished so much work as a Buddha? Was it through the authoritative powers of the Buddha, or through the blessings of the Buddha, that you were able to teach and convert such an immeasurable number of great bodhisattvas and enable them to achieve anuttara-samyak-sambodhi? World-Honored One, a multitude of great bodhisattvas such as this—a person might spend a thousand, ten thousand, a million kalpas counting them and never be able to reach the end or discover the limit! Since the far distant past, in the dwelling place of immeasurable, boundless numbers of Buddhas, they must have planted good roots, carried out the bodhisattva way, and engaged constantly in brahma practices. World-Honored One, it is hard for the world to believe such a thing!

"Suppose, for example, that a young man of twenty-five, with ruddy complexion and hair still black, should point to someone who was a hundred years old and say, 'This is my son!' or that the hundred year old man should point to the youth and say, 'This is my father who sired and raised me!' This would be hard to believe, and so too is what the Buddha says.

"It has in fact not been long since you attained the way. But this great multitude of bodhisattvas have already for immeasurable thousands, ten thousands, millions of kalpas applied themselves diligently and earnestly for the sake of the Buddha way. They have learned to enter into, emerge from and dwell in immeasurable hundreds, thousands, ten thousands, millions of samadhis, have acquired great transcendental powers, have over a long period carried out brahma practices, and have been able step by step to practice various good doctrines, becoming skilled in questions and answers, a treasure among persons, something seldom known in all the worlds. And today, World-Honored One, you tell us that, in the time since you attained the Buddha way, you have caused these persons for the first time to aspire to enlightenment, have taught, converted and led them, and directed them toward anuttara-samyak-sambodhi!

"World-Honored One, it is not long since you attained Buddhahood, and yet you have been able to carry out this great meritorious undertaking! We ourselves have faith in the Buddha, believing that he preaches in accordance with what is appropriate, that the words spoken by the Buddha are never false, and that the Buddha's knowledge is in all cases penetrating and comprehensive. Nevertheless, in the period after the Buddha has entered extinction, if bodhisattvas who have just begun to aspire to enlightenment should hear these words, they will perhaps not believe or accept them but will be led to commit the crime of rejecting the Law. Therefore, World-Honored One, we beg you to explain so we may put aside our doubts, and so that, in future ages when good men hear of this matter, they will not entertain doubts!"

At that time the bodhisattva Maitreya, wishing to state his meaning once more, spoke in verse form, saying:

> In the past the Buddha departed from the Shakya clan,
> left his household, and near Gaya
> sat under the bodhi tree.
> Little time has passed since then,
> yet these sons of the Buddha
> are immeasurable in number!
> Already for a long time they have practiced the Buddha way,
> dwelling in transcendental powers and the power of wisdom,
> skillfully learning the bodhisattva way,
> unsoiled by worldly things
> like the lotus flower in the water.
> Emerging from the earth,
> all display a reverent and respectful mind,
> standing in the presence of the World-Honored One.
> This is difficult to fathom—
> how can one believe it?
> The Buddha attained the way very recently,
> yet those he has helped to gain success are so many!
> We beg you to dispel the doubts of the assembly,
> to make distinctions and explain the truth of the matter.
> It is as though a young man
> just turned twenty-five
> were to point to a hundred year old man
> with gray hair and wrinkled face
> and say, 'I sired him!'
> and the old man were to say, 'This is my father!'

The father youthful, the son old—
no one in the world could believe this!
World-Honored One, your case is similar.
Only very recently you attained the way.
These bodhisattvas
are firm in will, in no way timid or immature.
For immeasurable kalpas
they have been practicing the bodhisattva way.
They are clever at difficult questions and answers,
their minds know no fear.
They have firmly cultivated a persevering mind,
upright in dignity and virtue.
They are praised by the Buddhas of the ten directions
as able and adept at preaching distinctions.
They have no wish to remain among the crowd
but constantly favor a state of meditation,
and in order to seek the Buddha way
they have been dwelling in the space under the earth.
This we have heard from the Buddha
and have no doubts in the matter.
But for the sake of future ages we beg the Buddha
to explain and bring about understanding.
If with regard to this sutra
one should harbor doubt and fail to believe,
he will fall at once into the evil paths.
So we beg you now to explain.
These immeasurable bodhisattvas—
how in such a short time
did you teach them, cause them to have aspiring minds,
and to dwell in the stage of no regression?

16

THE LIFE SPAN OF THE THUS COME ONE

At that time the Buddha spoke to the bodhisattvas and all the great assembly: "Good men, you must believe and understand the truthful words of the Thus Come One." And again he said to the great assembly: "You must believe and understand the truthful words of the Thus Come One." And once more he said to the great assembly: "You must believe and understand the truthful words of the Thus Come One."

At that time the bodhisattvas and the great assembly, with Maitreya as their leader, pressed their palms together and addressed the Buddha, saying: "World-Honored One, we beg you to explain. We will believe and accept the Buddha's words." They spoke in this manner three times, and then said once more: "We beg you to explain it. We will believe and accept the Buddha's words."

At that time the World-Honored One, seeing that the bodhisattvas repeated their request three times and more, spoke to them, saying: "You must listen carefully and hear of the Thus Come One's secret and his transcendental powers. In all the worlds the heavenly and human beings and asuras all believe that the present Shakyamuni Buddha, after leaving the palace of the Shakyas, seated himself in the place of practice not far from the city of Gaya and there attained anuttara-samyak-sambodhi. But good men, it has been immeasurable, boundless hundreds, thousands, ten thousands, millions of nayutas of kalpas since I in fact attained Buddhahood.

"Suppose a person were to take five hundred, a thousand, ten thousand, a million nayuta asamkhya thousand-millionfold worlds and grind them to dust. Then, moving eastward, each time he passes five hundred, a thousand, ten thousand, a million nayuta asamkhya worlds he drops a particle of dust. He continues eastward in this way until he has finished dropping all the particles. Good men, what is your opinion? Can the total number of all these worlds be imagined or calculated?"

The bodhisattva Maitreya and the others said to the Buddha: "World-Honored One, these worlds are immeasurable, boundless— one cannot calculate their number, nor does the mind have the power to encompass them. Even all the voice-hearers and pratyekabuddhas with their wisdom free of outflows could not imagine or understand how many there are. Although we abide in the stage of avivartika, we cannot comprehend such a matter. World-Honored One, these worlds are immeasurable and boundless."

At that time the Buddha said to the multitude of great bodhisattvas: "Good men, now I will state this to you clearly. Suppose all these worlds, whether they received a particle of dust or not, are once more reduced to dust. Let one particle represent one kalpa. The time that has passed since I attained Buddhahood surpasses this by a hundred, a thousand, ten thousand, a million nayuta asamkhya kalpas.

"Ever since then I have been constantly in this saha world, preaching the Law, teaching and converting. And elsewhere I have led and benefited living beings in hundreds, thousands, ten thousands, millions of nayutas and asamkhyas of lands.

"Good men, during that time I have spoken about the Buddha Burning Torch and others, and described how they entered nirvana. All this I employed as an expedient means to make distinctions.

"Good men, if there are living beings who come to me, I employ my Buddha eye to observe their faith and to see if their other faculties are keen or dull, and then depending upon how receptive they are to salvation, I appear in different places and preach to them under different names, and describe the length of time during which my teachings will be effective. Sometimes when I make my appearance I say that I am about to enter nirvana, and also employ different expedient means to preach the subtle and wonderful Law, thus causing living beings to awaken joyful minds.

"Good men, the Thus Come One observes how among living beings there are those who delight in a little Law, meager in virtue and heavy with defilement. For such persons I describe how in my youth I left my household and attained anuttara-samyak-sambodhi. But in truth the time since I attained Buddhahood is extremely long, as I have told you. It is simply that I use this expedient means to teach and convert living beings and cause them to enter the Buddha way. That is why I speak in this manner.

"Good men, the scriptures expounded by the Thus Come One are all for the purpose of saving and emancipating living beings. Sometimes I speak of myself, sometimes of others; sometimes I present myself, sometimes others; sometimes I show my own actions, sometimes those of others. All that I preach is true and not false.

"Why do I do this? The Thus Come One perceives the true aspect of the threefold world exactly as it is. There is no ebb or flow of birth and death, and there is no existing in this world and later entering extinction. It is neither substantial nor empty, neither consistent nor diverse. Nor is it what those who dwell in the threefold world perceive it to be. All such things the Thus Come One sees clearly and without error.

"Because living beings have different natures, different desires, different actions, and different ways of thinking and making distinctions, and because I want to enable them to put down good roots, I employ a variety of causes and conditions, similes, parables, and phrases and preach different doctrines. This, the Buddha's work, I have never for a moment neglected.

"Thus, since I attained Buddhahood, an extremely long period of time has passed. My life span is an immeasurable number of asamkhya kalpas, and during that time I have constantly abided here without ever entering extinction. Good men, originally I practiced the bodhisattva way, and the life span that I acquired then has yet to come to an end but will last twice the number of years that have already passed. Now, however, although in fact I do not actually enter extinction, I announce that I am going to adopt the course of extinction. This is an expedient means which the Thus Come One uses to teach and convert living beings.

"Why do I do this? Because if the Buddha remains in the world for a long time, those persons with shallow virtue will fail to plant good roots but, living in poverty and lowliness, will become attached to the five desires and be caught in the net of deluded thoughts and imaginings. If they see that the Thus Come One is constantly in the world and never enters extinction, they will grow arrogant and selfish, or become discouraged and neglectful. They will fail to realize how difficult it is to encounter the Buddha and will not approach him with a respectful and reverent mind.

"Therefore as an expedient means the Thus Come One says: 'Monks, you should know that it is a rare thing to live at a time when one of the Buddhas appears in the world.' Why does he do this? Because persons of shallow virtue may pass immeasurable hundreds, thousands, ten thousands, millions of kalpas with some of them chancing to see a Buddha and others never seeing one at all. For this reason I say to them: 'Monks, the Thus Come One is hard to get to see.' When living beings hear these words, they are certain to realize how difficult it is to encounter the Buddha. In their minds they will harbor a longing and will thirst to gaze upon the Buddha, and then they will work to plant good roots. Therefore the Thus Come One, though in truth he does not enter extinction, speaks of passing into extinction.

"Good men, the Buddhas and Thus Come Ones all preach a Law such as this. They act in order to save living beings, so what they do is true and not false.

"Suppose, for example, that there is a skilled physician who is wise and understanding and knows how to compound medicines to effectively cure all kinds of diseases. He has many sons, perhaps ten, twenty, or even a hundred. He goes off to some other land far away to see about a certain affair. After he has gone, the children drink some kind of poison that makes them distraught with pain and they fall writhing to the ground.

"At that time the father returns to his home and finds that his children have drunk poison. Some are completely out of their minds, while others are not. Seeing their father from far off, all are overjoyed and kneel down and entreat him, saying: 'How fine that you have returned safely. We were stupid and by mistake drank some poison. We beg you to cure us and let us live out our lives!'

"The father, seeing his children suffering like this, follows various prescriptions. Gathering fine medicinal herbs that meet all the requirements of color, fragrance and flavor, he grinds, sifts and mixes them together. Giving a dose of these to his children, he tells them: 'This is a highly effective medicine, meeting all the requirements of color, fragrance and flavor. Take it and you will quickly be relieved of your sufferings and will be free of all illness.'

"Those children who have not lost their senses can see that this is good medicine, outstanding in both color and fragrance, so they take it immediately and are completely cured of their sickness. Those who are out of their minds are equally delighted to see their father return and beg him to cure their sickness, but when they are given the medicine, they refuse to take it. Why? Because the poison has penetrated deeply and their minds no longer function as before. So although the medicine is of excellent color and fragrance, they do not perceive it as good.

"The father thinks to himself: My poor children! Because of the poison in them, their minds are completely befuddled. Although they are happy to see me and ask me to cure them, they refuse to take this excellent medicine. I must now resort to some expedient means to induce them to take the medicine. So he says to them: 'You should know that I am now old and worn out, and the time of my death has come. I will leave this good medicine here. You should take it and not worry that it will not cure you.' Having given these instructions, he then goes off to another land, where he sends a messenger home to announce, 'Your father is dead.'

"At that time the children, hearing that their father has deserted them and died, are filled with great grief and consternation and think to themselves: If our father were alive he would have pity on us and see that we are protected. But now he has abandoned us and died in some other country far away. We are shelterless orphans with no one to rely on!

"Constantly harboring such feelings of grief, they at last come to their senses and realize that the medicine is in fact excellent in color and fragrance and flavor, and so they take it and are healed of all the effects of the poison. The father, hearing that his children are all cured, immediately returns home and appears to them all once more.

"Good men, what is your opinion? Can anyone say that this skilled physician is guilty of lying?"

"No, World-Honored One."

The Buddha said: "It is the same with me. It has been immeasurable, boundless hundreds, thousands, ten thousands, millions of nayuta and asamkhya kalpas since I attained Buddhahood. But for the sake of living beings I employ the power of expedient means and say that I am about to pass into extinction. In view of the circumstances, however, no one can say that I have been guilty of lies or falsehoods."

At that time the World-Honored One, wishing to state his meaning once more, spoke in verse form, saying:

> Since I attained Buddhahood
> the number of kalpas that have passed
> is an immeasurable hundreds, thousands, ten thousands,
> millions, trillions, asamkhyas.
> Constantly I have preached the Law, teaching, converting
> countless millions of living beings,
> causing them to enter the Buddha way,
> all this for immeasurable kalpas.
> In order to save living beings,
> as an expedient means I appear to enter nirvana
> but in truth I do not pass into extinction.
> I am always here, preaching the Law.
> I am always here,
> but through my transcendental powers
> I make it so that living beings in their befuddlement
> do not see me even when close by.
> When the multitude see that I have passed into extinction,
> far and wide they offer alms to my relics.

All harbor thoughts of yearning
and in their minds thirst to gaze at me.
When living beings have become truly faithful,
honest and upright, gentle in intent,
single-mindedly desiring to see the Buddha,
not hesitating even if it costs them their lives,
then I and the assembly of monks
appear together on Holy Eagle Peak.
At that time I tell the living beings
that I am always here, never entering extinction,
but that because of the power of an expedient means
at times I appear to be extinct, at other times not,
and that if there are living beings in other lands
who are reverent and sincere in their wish to believe,
then among them too
I will preach the unsurpassed Law.
But you have not heard of this,
so you suppose that I enter extinction.
When I look at living beings
I see them drowned in a sea of suffering;
therefore I do not show myself,
causing them to thirst for me.
Then when their minds are filled with yearning,
at last I appear and preach the Law for them.
Such are my transcendental powers.
For asamkhya kalpas
constantly I have dwelled on Holy Eagle Peak
and in various other places.
When living beings witness the end of a kalpa
and all is consumed in a great fire,
this, my land, remains safe and tranquil,
constantly filled with heavenly and human beings.
The halls and pavilions in its gardens and groves
are adorned with various kinds of gems.
Jeweled trees abound in flowers and fruit
where living beings enjoy themselves at ease.
The gods strike heavenly drums,
constantly making many kinds of music.

Mandarava blossoms rain down,
  scattering over the Buddha and the great assembly.
My pure land is not destroyed,
  yet the multitude see it as consumed in fire,
with anxiety, fear and other sufferings
  filling it everywhere.
These living beings with their various offenses,
  through causes arising from their evil actions,
spend asamkhya kalpas
  without hearing the name of the Three Treasures.
But those who practice meritorious ways,
  who are gentle, peaceful, honest and upright,
all of them will see me
  here in person, preaching the Law.
At times for this multitude
  I describe the Buddha's life span as immeasurable,
and to those who see the Buddha only after a long time
  I explain how difficult it is to meet the Buddha.
Such is the power of my wisdom
  that its sagacious beams shine without measure.
This life span of countless kalpas
  I gained as the result of lengthy practice.
You who are possessed of wisdom,
  entertain no doubts on this point!
Cast them off, end them forever,
  for the Buddha's words are true, not false.
He is like a skilled physician
  who uses an expedient means to cure his deranged sons.
Though in fact alive, he gives out word he is dead,
  yet no one can say he speaks falsely.
I am the father of this world,
  saving those who suffer and are afflicted.
Because of the befuddlement of ordinary people,
  though I live, I give out word I have entered extinction.
For if they see me constantly,
  arrogance and selfishness arise in their minds.
Abandoning restraint, they give themselves up to the
    five desires

and fall into the evil paths of existence.
Always I am aware of which living beings
practice the way, and which do not,
and in response to their needs for salvation
I preach various doctrines for them.
At all times I think to myself:
How can I cause living beings
to gain entry into the unsurpassed way
and quickly acquire the body of a Buddha?

20

THE BODHISATTVA
NEVER DISPARAGING

At that time the Buddha said to the bodhisattva and mahasattva Gainer of Great Authority: "You should understand this. When monks, nuns, laymen or laywomen uphold the Lotus Sutra, if anyone should speak ill of them, curse or slander them, he will suffer severe recompense for his crime, as I have explained earlier. And I have also explained earlier the benefits gained by those who uphold the sutra, namely, purification of their eyes, ears, nose, tongue, body, and mind.

"Gainer of Great Authority, long ago, an immeasurable, boundless, inconceivable number of asamkhya kalpas in the past, there was a Buddha named Awesome Sound King Thus Come One, worthy of offerings, of right and universal knowledge, perfect clarity and conduct, well gone, understanding the world, unexcelled worthy, trainer of people, teacher of heavenly and human beings, Buddha, World-Honored One. His kalpa was called Exempt from Decay and his land was called Great Achievement.

"This Buddha Awesome Sound King during the age when he lived preached the Law for heavenly and human beings and asuras. For those who were seeking to become voice-hearers he responded by preaching the Law of the four noble truths so that they could transcend birth, old age, sickness and death and eventually attain nirvana. For those seeking to become pratyekabuddhas he responded by preaching the Law of the twelve-linked chain of causation. For the bodhisattvas, as a means to lead them to anuttara-samyak-sambodhi, he responded by preaching the Law of the six paramitas so that they could eventually gain the Buddha wisdom.

"Gainer of Great Authority, this Buddha Awesome Sound King had a life span of kalpas equal to four hundred thousand million nayutas of Ganges sands. His Correct Law endured in the world for as many kalpas as there are dust particles in one Jambudvipa. His Counterfeit Law endured in the world for as many kalpas as there are dust particles in the four continents. After this Buddha had finished bringing great benefit to living beings, he passed into extinction.

"After his Correct Law and Counterfeit Law had come to an end, another Buddha appeared in the same land. He too was named Awesome Sound King Thus Come One, worthy of offerings, of right and universal knowledge, perfect clarity and conduct, well gone, understanding the world, unexcelled worthy, trainer of people, teacher of heavenly and human beings, Buddha, World-Honored One. This process continued until twenty thousand million Buddhas had appeared one after the other, all bearing the same name.

"After the original Awesome Sound King Thus Come One had passed into extinction, and after his Correct Law had also passed away, in the period of his Counterfeit Law, monks of overbearing arrogance exercised great authority and power. At this time there was a bodhisattva monk named Never Disparaging. Now, Gainer of Great Authority, for what reason was he named Never Disparaging? This monk, whatever persons he happened to meet, whether monks, nuns, laymen or laywomen, would bow in obeisance to all of them and speak words of praise, saying, 'I have profound reverence for you, I would never dare treat you with disparagement or arrogance. Why? Because you are all practicing the bodhisattva way and are certain to attain Buddhahood.'

"This monk did not devote his time to reading or reciting the scriptures, but simply went about bowing to people. And if he happened to see any of the four kinds of believers far off in the distance, he would purposely go to where they were, bow to them and speak words of praise, saying, 'I would never dare disparage you, because you are all certain to attain Buddhahood!'

"Among the four kinds of believers there were those who gave way to anger, their minds lacking in purity, and they spoke ill of him and cursed him, saying, 'This ignorant monk—where does he come from, presuming to declare that he does not disparage us and bestowing on us a prediction that we will attain Buddhahood? We have no use for such vain and irresponsible predictions!'

"Many years passed in this way, during which this monk was constantly subjected to curses and abuse. He did not give way to anger, however, but each time spoke the same words, 'You are certain to attain Buddhahood.' When he spoke in this manner, some among the group would take sticks of wood or tiles and stones and beat and pelt him. But even as he ran away and took up his stance at a distance, he continued to call out in a loud voice, 'I would never dare disparage you, for you are all certain to attain Buddhahood!' And because he always spoke these words, the overbearingly arrogant monks, nuns, laymen and laywomen gave him the name Never Disparaging.

"When this monk was on the point of death, he heard up in the sky fully twenty thousand, ten thousand, a million verses of the Lotus Sutra that had previously been preached by the Buddha Awesome Sound King, and he was able to accept and uphold them all. Immediately he gained the kind of purity of vision and purity of the faculties of the ear, nose, tongue, body and mind that have been described above. Having gained this purity of the six faculties, his life span was increased by two hundred ten thousand million nayutas of years, and he went about widely preaching the Lotus Sutra for people.

"At that time, when the four kinds of believers who were overbearingly arrogant, the monks, nuns, laymen and laywomen who had looked with contempt on this monk and given him the name Never Disparaging—when they saw that he had gained great transcendental powers, the power to preach pleasingly and eloquently, the power of great goodness and tranquility, and when they heard his preaching, they all took faith in him and willingly became his followers.

"This bodhisattva converted a multitude of a thousand, ten thousand, a million, causing them to abide in the state of anuttara-samyak-sambodhi. After his life came to an end, he was able to encounter two thousand million Buddhas, all bearing the name Sun Moon Bright, and in the midst of their Law he preached this Lotus Sutra. Through the causes and conditions created thereby, he was also able to encounter two thousand million Buddhas, all with the identical name Cloud Freedom Lamp King. In the midst of the Law of these Buddhas, he accepted, upheld, read, recited and preached this sutra for the four kinds of believers. For that reason he was able to gain purification of his ordinary eyes, and the faculties of his ears, nose, tongue, body and mind were likewise purified. Among the four kinds of believers he preached the Law with no fear in his mind.

"Gainer of Great Authority, this bodhisattva and mahasattva Never Disparaging in this manner offered alms to a vast number of Buddhas, treating them with reverence and honor and praising them. Having planted these good roots, he was later able to encounter a thousand, ten thousand, a million Buddhas, and in the midst of the Law of these Buddhas, he preached this sutra, gaining benefits that allowed him to attain Buddhahood.

"Gainer of Great Authority, what do you think? The bodhisattva Never Disparaging who lived at that time—could he be unknown to you? In fact he was none other than I myself! If in my previous existences I had not accepted, upheld, read and recited this sutra and preached it for others, I would never have been able to attain anuttara-samyak-sambodhi this quickly. Because in the presence of those earlier Buddhas I accepted, upheld, read and recited this sutra and preached it for others, I was able quickly to attain anuttara-samyak-sambodhi.

"Gainer of Great Authority, at that time the four kinds of believers, the monks, nuns, laymen and laywomen, because anger arose in their minds and they treated me with disparagement and contempt, were for two hundred million kalpas never able to encounter a Buddha, to hear the Law, or to see the community of monks. For a thousand kalpas they underwent great suffering in the Avichi hell. After they had finished paying for their offenses, they once more encountered the bodhisattva Never Disparaging, who instructed them in anuttara-samyak-sambodhi.

"Gainer of Great Authority, what do you think? The four kinds of believers who at that time constantly disparaged this bodhisattva—could they be unknown to you? They are in this assembly now, Bhadrapala and his group, five hundred bodhisattvas; Lion Moon and her group, five hundred nuns; and Thinking of Buddha and his group, five hundred laymen, all having reached the state where they will never regress in their search for anuttara-samyak-sambodhi!

"Gainer of Great Authority, you should understand that this Lotus Sutra richly benefits the bodhisattvas and mahasattvas, for it can cause them to attain anuttara-samyak-sambodhi. For this reason, after the Thus Come One has passed into extinction, the bodhisattvas and mahasattvas should at all times accept, uphold, read, recite, explain, preach and transcribe this sutra."

At that time the World-Honored One, wishing to state his meaning once more, spoke in verse form, saying:

> In the past there was a Buddha
> named Awesome Sound King,
> of immeasurable supernatural powers and wisdom,
> leading and guiding one and all.
> Heavenly and human beings, dragons, spirits
> joined in offering him alms.
> After this Buddha had entered extinction,
> when his Law was about to expire,
> there was a bodhisattva
> named Never Disparaging.
> The four kinds of believers at that time
> scrutinized and adhered to the Law.
> The bodhisattva Never Disparaging
> would go to where they were
> and speak to them, saying,
> "I would never disparage you,
> for you are practicing the way
> and all of you will become Buddhas!"
> When the people heard this,
> they gibed at him, cursed and reviled him,

but the bodhisattva Never Disparaging
bore all this with patience.
When his offenses had been wiped out
and his life was drawing to a close,
he was able to hear this sutra
and his six faculties were purified.
Because of his transcendental powers
his life span was extended,
and for the sake of others
he preached this sutra far and wide.
The many persons who adhered to the Law
all received teaching and conversion
from this bodhisattva,
who caused them to dwell in the Buddha way.
When Never Disparaging's life ended,
he encountered numberless Buddhas,
and because he preached this sutra
he gained immeasurable blessings.
Bit by bit he acquired benefits
and quickly completed the Buddha way.
Never Disparaging who lived at that time
was none other than myself.
And the four kinds of believers
who adhered to the Law then,
who heard Never Disparaging say,
"You will become Buddhas!"
and through the causes thus created
encountered numberless Buddhas—
they are here in this assembly,
a group of five hundred bodhisattvas,
and the four kinds of believers,
men and women of pure faith
who now in my presence
listen to the Law.
In previous existences
I encouraged these persons
to listen to and accept this sutra,
the foremost in the Law,

unfolding it, teaching people,
and causing them to dwell in nirvana.
So in age after age they accepted and upheld
scriptures of this kind.
A million million ten thousand kalpas,
an inconceivable time will pass
before at last one can hear
this Lotus Sutra.
A million million ten thousand kalpas,
an inconceivable time will pass
before the Buddhas, World-Honored Ones,
preach this sutra.
Therefore its practitioners,
after the Buddha has entered extinction,
when they hear a sutra like this
should entertain no doubts or perplexities
but should with a single mind
preach this sutra far and wide,
age after age encountering Buddhas
and quickly completing the Buddha way.

22

ENTRUSTMENT

At that time Shakyamuni Buddha rose from his Dharma seat and, manifesting his great supernatural powers, with his right hand patted the heads of the immeasurable bodhisattvas and mahasattvas and spoke these words: "For immeasurable hundreds, thousands, ten thousands, millions of asamkhya kalpas I have practiced this hard-to-attain Law of anuttara-samyak-sambodhi. Now I entrust it to you. You must single-mindedly propagate this Law abroad, causing its benefits to spread far and wide."

Three times he patted the bodhisattvas and mahasattvas on the head and spoke these words: "For immeasurable hundreds, thousands, ten thousands, millions of asamkhya kalpas I have practiced this hard-to-attain Law of anuttara-samyak-sambodhi. Now I entrust it to you. You must accept, uphold, read, recite, and broadly propagate this Law, causing all living beings everywhere to hear and understand it. Why? Because the Thus Come One has great pity and compassion. He is in no way stingy or begrudging, nor has he any fear. He is able to bestow on living beings the wisdom of the Buddha, the wisdom of the Thus Come One, the wisdom that comes of itself. The Thus Come One is a great giver of gifts to all living beings. You for your part should respond by studying this Law of the Thus Come One. You must not be stingy or begrudging!

"In future ages if there are good men and good women who have faith in the wisdom of the Thus Come One, you should preach and expound the Lotus Sutra for them, so that others may hear and understand it. For in this way you can cause them to gain the Buddha wisdom. If there are living beings who do not believe and accept it, you should use some of the other profound doctrines of the Thus Come One to teach, benefit and bring joy to them. If you do all this, then you will have repaid the debt of gratitude that you owe to the Buddhas."

When the bodhisattvas and mahasattvas heard the Buddha speak these words, they all experienced a great joy that filled their bodies. With even greater reverence than before, they bent their bodies, bowed their heads, pressed their palms together and, facing the Buddha, raised their voices in unison, saying: "We will respectfully carry out all these things just as the World-Honored One has commanded. We beg the World-Honored One to have no concern on this account!"

The multitude of bodhisattvas and mahasattvas repeated these words three times, raising their voices in unison and saying: "We will respectfully carry out all these things just as the World-Honored One has commanded. Therefore we beg the World-Honored One to have no concern on this account!"

At that time Shakyamuni Buddha caused the Buddhas who were emanations of his body and had come from the ten directions to return each one to his original land, saying: "Each of these Buddhas may proceed at his own pleasure. The tower of Many Treasures Buddha may also return to its former position."

When he spoke these words, the immeasurable emanation Buddhas from the ten directions who were seated on lion seats under the jeweled trees, as well as Many Treasures Buddha, Superior Practices, and the others of the great multitude of boundless asamkhyas of bodhisattvas, Shariputra and the other voice-hearers and four kinds of believers, and the heavenly and human beings, asuras and others in all the worlds, hearing what the Buddha had said, were all filled with great joy.

25

THE UNIVERSAL GATEWAY OF THE BODHISATTVA PERCEIVER OF THE WORLD'S SOUNDS

At that time the bodhisattva Inexhaustible Intent immediately rose from his seat, bared his right shoulder, pressed his palms together and, facing the Buddha, spoke these words: "World-Honored One, this Bodhisattva Perceiver of the World's Sounds—why is he called Perceiver of the World's Sounds?"

The Buddha said to Bodhisattva Inexhaustible Intent: "Good man, suppose there are immeasurable hundreds, thousands, ten thousands, millions of living beings who are undergoing various trials and suffering. If they hear of this bodhisattva Perceiver of the World's Sounds and single-mindedly call his name, then at once he will perceive the sound of their voices and they will all gain deliverance from their trials.

"If someone, holding fast to the name of Bodhisattva Perceiver of the World's Sounds, should enter a great fire, the fire could not burn him. This would come about because of this bodhisattva's authority and supernatural power. If one were washed away by a great flood and called upon his name, one would immediately find himself in a shallow place.

"Suppose there were a hundred, a thousand, ten thousand, a million living beings who, seeking for gold, silver, lapis lazuli, seashell, agate, coral, amber, pearls, and other treasures, set out on the great sea. And suppose a fierce wind should blow their ship off course and it drifted to the land of rakshasa demons. If among those people there is even just one who calls the name of Bodhisattva Perceiver of the World's Sounds, then all those people will be delivered from their troubles with the rakshasas. This is why he is called Perceiver of the World's Sounds.

"If a person who faces imminent threat of attack should call the name of Bodhisattva Perceiver of the World's Sounds, then the swords and staves wielded by his attackers would instantly shatter into so many pieces and he would be delivered.

"Though enough yakshas and rakshasas to fill all the thousand-millionfold world should try to come and torment a person, if they hear him calling the name of Bodhisattva Perceiver of the World's Sounds, then these evil demons will not even be able to look at him with their evil eyes, much less do him harm.

"Suppose there is a person who, whether guilty or not guilty, has had his body imprisoned in fetters and chains, cangue and lock. If he calls the name of Bodhisattva Perceiver of the World's Sounds, then all his bonds will be severed and broken and at once he will gain deliverance.

"Suppose, in a place filled with all the evil-hearted bandits of the thousand-millionfold world, there is a merchant leader who is guiding a band of merchants carrying valuable treasures over a steep and dangerous road, and that one man shouts out these words: 'Good men, do not be afraid! You must single-mindedly call on the name of Bodhisattva Perceiver of the World's Sounds. This bodhisattva can grant fearlessness to living beings. If you call his name, you will be delivered from these evil-hearted bandits!' When the band of merchants hear this, they all together raise their voices, saying, 'Hail to the Bodhisattva Perceiver of the World's Sounds!' And because they call his name, they are at once able to gain deliverance. Inexhaustible Intent, the authority and supernatural power of the bodhisattva and mahasattva Perceiver of the World's Sounds are as mighty as this!

"If there should be living beings beset by numerous lusts and cravings, let them think with constant reverence of Bodhisattva Perceiver of the World's Sounds and then they can shed their desires. If they have great wrath and ire, let them think with constant reverence of Bodhisattva Perceiver of the World's Sounds and then they can shed their ire. If they have great ignorance and stupidity, let them think with constant reverence of Bodhisattva Perceiver of the World's Sounds and they can rid themselves of stupidity.

"Inexhaustible Intent, the bodhisattva Perceiver of the World's Sounds possesses great authority and supernatural powers, as I have described, and can confer many benefits. For this reason, living beings should constantly keep the thought of him in mind.

"If a woman wishes to give birth to a male child, she should offer obeisance and alms to Bodhisattva Perceiver of the World's Sounds and then she will bear a son blessed with merit, virtue, and wisdom. And if she wishes to bear a daughter, she will bear one with all the marks of comeliness, one who in the past planted the roots of virtue and is loved and respected by many persons.

"Inexhaustible Intent, the bodhisattva Perceiver of the World's Sounds has power to do all this. If there are living beings who pay respect and obeisance to Bodhisattva Perceiver of the World's Sounds, their good fortune will not be fleeting or vain. Therefore living beings should all accept and uphold the name of Bodhisattva Perceiver of the World's Sounds.

"Inexhaustible Intent, suppose there is a person who accepts and upholds the names of as many bodhisattvas as there are sands in sixty-two million Ganges, and for as long as his present body lasts, he offers them alms in the form of food and drink, clothing, bedding and medicines. What is your opinion? Would this good man or good woman gain many benefits, or would he not?"

Inexhaustible Intent replied, "They would be very many, World-Honored One."

The Buddha said: "Suppose also that there is a person who accepts and upholds the name of Bodhisattva Perceiver of the World's Sounds and even just once offers him obeisance and alms. The good fortune gained by these two persons would be exactly equal and without difference. For a hundred, a thousand, ten thousand, a million kalpas it would never be exhausted or run out. Inexhaustible Intent, if one accepts and upholds the name of Bodhisattva Perceiver of the World's Sounds, he will gain the benefit of merit and virtue that is as immeasurable and boundless as this!"

Bodhisattva Inexhaustible Intent said to the Buddha, "World-Honored One, Bodhisattva Perceiver of the World's Sounds—how does he come and go in this saha world? How does he preach the Law for the sake of living beings? How does the power of expedient means apply in his case?"

The Buddha said to Bodhisattva Inexhaustible Intent: "Good man, if there are living beings in the land who need someone in the body of a Buddha in order to be saved, Bodhisattva Perceiver of the World's Sounds immediately manifests himself in a Buddha body and preaches the Law for them. If they need someone in a pratyekabuddha's body in order to be saved, immediately he manifests a pratyekabuddha's body and preaches the Law to them. If they need a voice-hearer to be saved, immediately he becomes a voice-hearer and preaches the Law for them. If they need King Brahma to be saved, immediately he becomes King Brahma and preaches the Law for them. If they need the lord Shakra to be saved, immediately he becomes the lord Shakra and preaches the Law for them. If they need the heavenly being Freedom to be saved, immediately he becomes the heavenly being Freedom and preaches the Law for them. If they need the heavenly being Great Freedom to be saved, immediately he becomes the heavenly being Great Freedom and preaches the Law for them. If they need a great general of heaven to be saved, immediately he becomes a great general of heaven and preaches the Law for them. If they need Vaishravana to be saved, immediately he becomes Vaishravana and preaches the Law for them. If they need a petty king to be saved, immediately he becomes a petty king and preaches the Law for them. If they need a rich man to be saved, immediately he becomes a rich man and preaches the Law for them. If they need a householder to be saved, immediately he becomes a householder and preaches the Law for them.

If they need a chief minister to be saved, immediately he becomes a chief minister and preaches the Law for them. If they need a Brahman to be saved, immediately he becomes a Brahman and preaches the Law for them. If they need a monk, a nun, a layman believer, or a lay-woman believer to be saved, immediately he becomes a monk, a nun, a layman believer, or a laywoman believer and preaches the Law for them. If they need the wife of a rich man, of a householder, a chief minister, or a Brahman to be saved, immediately he becomes those wives and preaches the Law for them. If they need a young boy or a young girl to be saved, immediately he becomes a young boy or a young girl and preaches the Law for them. If they need a heavenly being, a dragon, a yaksha, a gandharva, an asura, a garuda, a kimnara, a mahoraga, a human or a nonhuman being to be saved, immediately he becomes all of these and preaches the Law for them. If they need a vajra-bearing god to be saved, immediately he becomes a vajra-bearing god and preaches the Law for them.

"Inexhaustible Intent, this Bodhisattva Perceiver of the World's Sounds has succeeded in acquiring benefits such as these and, taking on a variety of different forms, goes about among the lands saving living beings. For this reason you and the others should single-mindedly offer alms to Bodhisattva Perceiver of the World's Sounds. This bodhisattva and mahasattva Perceiver of the World's Sounds can bestow fearlessness on those who are in fearful, pressing or difficult circumstances. That is why in this saha world everyone calls him Bestower of Fearlessness."

Bodhisattva Inexhaustible Intent said to the Buddha, "World-Honored One, now I must offer alms to Bodhisattva Perceiver of the World's Sounds."

Then he took from his neck a necklace adorned with numerous precious gems, worth a hundred or a thousand taels of gold, and presented it to [the bodhisattva], saying, "Sir, please accept this necklace of precious gems as a gift in the Dharma."

At that time Bodhisattva Perceiver of the World's Sounds was unwilling to accept the gift.

Inexhaustible Intent spoke once more to Bodhisattva Perceiver of the World's Sounds, saying, "Sir, out of compassion for us, please accept this necklace."

Then the Buddha said to Bodhisattva Perceiver of the World's

Sounds, "Out of compassion for this bodhisattva Inexhaustible Intent and for the four kinds of believers, the heavenly beings, dragons, yakshas, gandharvas, asuras, garudas, kimnaras, mahoragas, human and nonhuman beings, you should accept this necklace."

Thereupon Bodhisattva Perceiver of the World's Sounds, having compassion for the four kinds of believers and the heavenly beings, dragons, human and nonhuman beings and the others, accepted the necklace and, dividing it into two parts, presented one part to Shakyamuni Buddha and presented the other to the tower of the Buddha Many Treasures.

[The Buddha said,] "Inexhaustible Intent, these are the kinds of freely exercised supernatural powers that Bodhisattva Perceiver of the World's Sounds displays in his comings and goings in the saha world."

At that time Bodhisattva Inexhaustible Intent posed this question in verse form:

> World-Honored One replete with wonderful features,
> I now ask you once again
> for what reason that Buddha's son
> is named Perceiver of the World's Sounds?
> The Honored One endowed with wonderful features
> replied to Inexhaustible Intent in verse:
> Listen to the actions of the Perceiver of Sounds,
> how aptly he responds in various quarters.
> His vast oath is deep as the ocean;
> kalpas pass but it remains unfathomable.
> He has attended many thousands and millions of Buddhas,
> setting forth his great pure vow.
> I will describe him in outline for you—
> listen to his name, observe his body,
> bear him in mind, not passing the time vainly,
> for he can wipe out the pains of existence.
> Suppose someone should conceive a wish to harm you,
> should push you into a great pit of fire.
> Think on the power of that Perceiver of Sounds
> and the pit of fire will change into a pond!
> If you should be cast adrift on the vast ocean,
> menaced by dragons, fish and various demons,

think on the power of that Perceiver of Sounds
and the billows and waves cannot drown you!
Suppose you are on the peak of Mount Sumeru
and someone pushes you off.
Think on the power of that Perceiver of Sounds
and you will hang in midair like the sun!
Suppose you are pursued by evil men
who wish to throw you down from a diamond mountain.
Think on the power of the Perceiver of Sounds
and they cannot harm a hair of you!
Suppose you are surrounded by evil-hearted bandits,
each brandishing a knife to wound you.
Think on the power of that Perceiver of Sounds
and at once all will be swayed by compassion!
Suppose you encounter trouble with the king's law,
face punishment, about to forfeit your life.
Think on the power of that Perceiver of Sounds
and the executioner's sword will be broken to bits!
Suppose you are imprisoned in cangue and lock,
hands and feet bound by fetters and chains.
Think on the power of that Perceiver of Sounds
and they will fall off, leaving you free!
Suppose with curses and various poisonous herbs
someone should try to injure you.
Think on the power of that Perceiver of Sounds
and the injury will rebound upon the originator.
Suppose you encounter evil rakshasas,
poison dragons and various demons.
Think on the power of that Perceiver of Sounds
and then none of them will dare to harm you.
If evil beasts should encircle you,
their sharp fangs and claws inspiring terror,
think on the power of that Perceiver of Sounds
and they will scamper away in boundless retreat.
If lizards, snakes, vipers, scorpions
threaten you with poison breath that sears like flame,
think on the power of that Perceiver of Sounds
and, hearing your voice, they will flee of themselves.

If clouds should bring thunder, and lightning strike,
if hail pelts or drenching rain comes down,
think on the power of that Perceiver of Sounds
and at that moment they will vanish away.
If living beings encounter weariness or peril,
immeasurable suffering pressing them down,
the power of the Perceiver of Sounds' wonderful wisdom
can save them from the sufferings of the world.
He is endowed with transcendental powers
and widely practices the expedient means of wisdom.
Throughout the lands in the ten directions
there is no region where he does not manifest himself.
In many different kinds of evil circumstances,
in the realms of hell, hungry spirits or beasts,
the sufferings of birth, old age, sickness and death—
all these he bit by bit wipes out.
He of the true gaze, the pure gaze,
the gaze of great and encompassing wisdom,
the gaze of pity, the gaze of compassion—
constantly we implore him, constantly look up in reverence.
His pure light, free of blemish,
is a sun of wisdom dispelling all darknesses.
He can quell the wind and fire of misfortune
and everywhere bring light to the world.
The precepts from his compassionate body shake us
    like thunder,
the wonder of his pitying mind is like a great cloud.
He sends down the sweet dew, the Dharma rain,
to quench the flames of earthly desires.
When law suits bring you before the officials,
when terrified in the midst of an army,
think on the power of that Perceiver of Sounds
and hatred in all its forms will be dispelled.
Wonderful sound, Perceiver of the World's Sounds,
Brahma's sound, the sea tide sound—
they surpass those sounds of the world;
therefore you should constantly think on them,
from thought to thought never entertaining doubt!

Perceiver of the World's Sounds, pure sage—
to those in suffering, in danger of death,
he can offer aid and support.
Endowed with all benefits,
he views living beings with compassionate eyes.
The sea of his accumulated blessings is immeasurable;
therefore you should bow your head to him!

At that time the bodhisattva Earth Holder immediately rose from his seat, advanced, and said to the Buddha, "World-Honored One, if there are living beings who hear this chapter on Bodhisattva Perceiver of the World's Sounds, on the freedom of his actions, his manifestation of a universal gateway, and his transcendental powers, it should be known that the benefits these persons gain are not few!"

When the Buddha preached this chapter on the Universal Gateway, a multitude of eighty-four thousand persons in the assembly all conceived a determination to attain the unparalleled state of anuttara-samyak-sambodhi.

GLOSSARY

The Glossary contains definitions of all important personal and place names appearing in the translation, as well as major Sanskrit terms and numerical categories. A few names of very minor figures and some Sanskrit names of flowers, birds, types of perfume, etc., that appear only once or twice in the text have been omitted. Sanskrit words are given with full diacritical marks when that form differs from the one in which the word appears in the translation: Skt = Sanskrit; Ch = Chinese; J = Japanese.

Ajatashatru (Ajātaśatru). A king of the state of Magadha in Shakyamuni's time. He made Magadha into the most powerful kingdom in India at that period. Later in his life he converted to Buddhism.

Ajnata Kaundinya (Ājñāta Kauṇḍinya). One of the five ascetics who heard Shakyamuni's first sermon and converted to his teachings. The eighth chapter of the Lotus Sutra predicts that he will become a Buddha named Universal Brightness.

Akanishtha (Akaniṣṭha). The highest heaven in the world of form. Beings living in this heaven possess a pure body, free from all suffering and illness.

Akshobhya (Akṣobhya). A Buddha mentioned in the seventh chapter of the Lotus Sutra. He became an important figure in esoteric Buddhism.

Amitayus (Amitāyus). A Buddha mentioned in chapters seven and twenty-three of the Lotus Sutra. Also known as Amitābha, he became the central figure in the Pure Land teachings of Chinese and Japanese Buddhism.

anagamin (anāgāmin). One of the four kinds of shravakas or voice-hearers. The anagamin is a voice-hearer who does not have to return to the world of human beings anymore.

Ananda (Ānanda). A cousin of Shakyamuni and one of his ten major disciples. He accompanied Shakyamuni for many years as his personal attendant and heard more of his teachings than any other disciple. He is accordingly known as foremost in hearing the Buddha's teachings. At the First Council held after Shakyamuni's death to put in order his teachings, Ananda is said to have recited the sutras from memory. The words "This is what I heard" that appear at the beginning of most sutras refer to this recitation.

Aniruddha (also called Anuruddha). A cousin of Shakyamuni and one of his ten major disciples, known as foremost in divine insight. The eighth chapter of the Lotus Sutra predicts that he will become a Buddha named Universal Brightness.

anuttara-samyak-sambodhi (anuttara-samyak-saṃbodhi). Supreme perfect enlightenment, the enlightenment of a Buddha.

arhat. A "worthy," one who has attained the highest stage of Hinayana enlightenment, the highest among the four kinds of shravakas or voice-hearers. Such a person has gained freedom from transmigration in the six paths of existence. The Lotus Sutra urges one to reject the goal of arhat and instead strive for the highest level of enlightenment, that of Buddhahood.

asamkhya (asaṃkhya). An ancient Indian numerical unit, indicating an uncountably large number.

Asita. The name of a seer who in a later existence became Devadatta, as related in the twelfth chapter of the Lotus Sutra.

asura. A class of contentious demons in Indian mythology who fight continually with the god Indra. In Buddhism the asuras constitute one of the eight kinds of nonhuman beings who protect Buddhism.

Avichi (Avīci). The hell of incessant suffering, the most terrible of the eight hot hells. One who commits one of the five cardinal sins or slanders the True Law is said to fall into this hell.

avivartika. Also rendered as avaivartika. Terms for the stage at which one is certain never to regress in religious practice, or for a person who has reached that stage.

Bhadrapala (Bhadrapāla). A bodhisattva who was among the assembly described in chapter one of the Lotus Sutra.

bodhi. Enlightenment or Buddhahood.

bodhi tree. The pipal tree at Buddhagayā under which Shakyamuni attained enlightenment.

bodhisattva. A being who aspires to attain Buddhahood and carries out various altruistic practices in order to achieve that goal. Compassion is the outstanding characteristic of the bodhisattva, who postpones his or her own entry into nirvana in order to assist others to gain enlightenment. The bodhisattva figure is particularly important in Mahayana Buddhism.

Brahma (Brahmā). Also called Mahābrahman. An Indian deity regarded as the personification of the fundamental universal principle. In Buddhism he was adopted as a protective deity. He lives in the first of the four meditation heavens in the world of form above Mt. Sumeru and rules the saha world.

Brahma (Brahmā) heaven. Another name for the first of the four meditation heavens in the world of form.

Brahma (Brahmā) king. A king of the Brahma heaven, a deity who has attained supremacy in a particular universe. In the Lotus Sutra a great number of Brahma kings appear.

brahma practices. Religious practices of a pure nature.

brahma sound. 1. A pure sound or pure voice. 2. The voice of a Brahma king.

Brahman. A member of the priestly class, the highest of the four classes in ancient Indian society.

Buddha. An "awakened one," one who has reached the highest level of enlightenment. In Mahayana Buddhism, the number of Buddhas is infinite, but the term often refers specifically to Shakyamuni Buddha, the Buddha of our present saha world.

chandala (caṇḍāla). An untouchable class, below the lowest of the four classes in ancient India. People in this class handled corpses, butchered animals, and carried out other tasks associated with the killing of living creatures.

Correct Law (Ch cheng-fa, J shōbō). According to Buddhist belief, after the death of a Buddha, his teachings pass through three periods or phases of development. In the first, known as the period of the Correct Law, Buddhism is a living religion and those who practice it attain enlightenment through its teachings. The period of the Correct Law following the death of Shakyamuni Buddha is usually said to be a thousand years in length, though some sources describe it as five hundred years long. *See also* Counterfeit Law *and* Latter Day of the Law.

Counterfeit Law (Ch hsiang-fa, J zōbō). Second period following the death of a Buddha. During this period, Buddhism becomes increasingly formalized, people's connection with it weakens, and progressively fewer of them are able to gain enlightenment through its teachings. Some sources describe the period of the Counterfeit Law following Shakyamuni's death as a thousand years in length, others as five hundred years.

Devadatta. A disciple of Shakyamuni and, according to some sources, Shakyamuni's cousin. He was at first diligent in religious practice but later, growing envious of Shakyamuni, worked to foment dissension within the Order and made several attempts on Shakyamuni's life. He is regarded as the epitome of evil and is said to have fallen into hell alive, but chapter twelve of the Lotus Sutra predicts that he will attain Buddhahood in a future existence.

dharani (dhāraṇī). A spell or formula said to protect the one who recites it and benefit the person by virtue of its mystic power.

dharma (Ch fa, J hō). 1. The Law or body of the Buddhist teachings; when this meaning is intended, the word has been translated as Law or written as Dharma. 2. Phenomena, things, facts, existences, as in the phrase "the true aspect of all phenomena" (Ch chu-fa shih-hsiang, J shohō jissō).

Dharma King. A term for the Buddha.

Dharma prince, A term for a bodhisattva.

Dharma seal. The emblem of the Law or essence of the Buddha's teachings.

dhuta (dhūta). A discipline or ascetic practice carried out in order to purify the body and mind and free one from the desire for food, clothing and shelter.

dragon (Skt nāga, Ch lung, J ryū). One of the eight kinds of nonhuman beings who protect Buddhism and appear frequently in the Lotus Sutra. The first chapter of the Lotus Sutra lists eight dragon kings who attended the preaching of the sutra.

eighteen unshared properties. Properties possessed by a Buddha and not shared by others. They are freedom from illusions, eloquence, absence of attachments, impartiality, constant concentration of mind, knowledge of all things, untiring intention to lead people to salvation, incessant endeavor, consistency of teachings with those of other Buddhas, perfect wisdom, perfect emancipation, perfect insight, consistency of deeds with wisdom, consistency of words with wisdom, consistency of mind with wisdom, knowledge of the past, knowledge of the future, and knowledge of the present.

eight emancipations. They are emancipation from the view that the body is pure, from the view that the outside world is pure, from illusions, from the view that matter exists, from the view that consciousness has limits, from the view that a thing has its own property, from the view that thought exists or that thought does not exist, and from the view that mentality exists in any sense.

eighty characteristics. Extraordinary features which only Buddhas and bodhisattvas possess. There are various explanations of the eighty characteristics; some of the characteristics duplicate the thirty-two features.

evil paths of existence. The three lowest of the six paths or realms in which unenlightened beings transmigrate. They are hell, the realm of hungry spirits, and that of beasts. Sometimes the realm of the asuras is included to make four evil paths.

expedient means (Skt upāya, Ch fang-pien, J hōben). A device or temporary means adopted in order to relieve suffering and lead beings to enlightenment, often by offering provisional teachings as a means of guiding them to the truth. It is the title of the second chapter of the Lotus Sutra.

five ascetics. Five men whom Shakyamuni's father sent to accompany Shakyamuni when he embarked on ascetic practices. Later, when Shakyamuni forsook extreme asceticism, they thought he had abandoned the search for truth and accordingly left him. After Shakyamuni had attained enlightenment, he sought them out and preached to them at the Deer Park in Varanasi, converting them to his teachings. One of them was Ajnata Kaundinya, who is mentioned in the Lotus Sutra.

five components. Also called the five skandas. Form, perception, conception, volition, and consciousness.

five desires. The desires that arise from the contact of the five sense organs, eyes, ears, nose, tongue, and body, with their respective objects. Sometimes the five desires are defined as the desire for wealth, sex, food and drink, fame, and sleep.

five emotions. Another term for the five desires.

five impurities. Sometimes called the five defilements; they are (1) the impurity of the age, such as war or other disruptions of the social or natural environment; (2) impurity of desire, the tendency to be ruled by emotions such as greed or anger; (3) impurity of living beings, the physical and spiritual decline of human beings; (4) impurity of view, impurity deriving from mistaken views or values; and (5) impurity of life span, the distortion of life itself, which leads to a disordered and shortened life span.

five obstacles. Five limitations set forth in some Buddhist teachings which women face in their religious practice. According to this view, a woman can never become a Brahma heavenly king, can never become the lord Shakra, can never become a devil king, can never become a wheel-turning sage king, and can never become a Buddha. In chapter twelve of the Lotus Sutra, this view is refuted.

five transcendental powers. The first five of the six transcendental powers; see six transcendental powers.

four elements. The four basic elements which according to ancient Indian belief make up all things. They are earth, water, fire, and wind. In addition to these, Buddhism postulates a fifth element, emptiness or space, which serves to integrate and harmonize the four elements.

Four Heavenly Kings. Lords of the four quarters who serve Indra as his generals and protect the four continents. They are Dhrtarāṣṭra, who appears in the Lotus Sutra under the name Upholder of the Nation, guardian of the east; Virūḍhaka, guardian of the south; Virūpākṣa, who guards the west; and Vaiśravaṇa, who guards the north.

four kinds of believers. Monks, nuns, laymen, and laywomen.

four kinds of fearlessness. Four aspects of the Buddha's fearlessness in preaching. The Buddha is fearless in declaring that he is enlightened to the truth of all phenomena; fearless in proclaiming he has extinguished all desires and illusions; fearless in teaching that desires and karma can be obstacles to enlightenment; and fearless in teaching that one can overcome all sufferings by practicing Buddhism.

four kinds of offerings to the community of monks. Clothing, food and drink, bedding, and medicine.

four methods of winning people. Four methods employed by bodhisattvas to attract others to their teachings. They are to give alms and expound the Law; to speak in a kindly manner; to work to benefit others; and to share their hardships and cooperate with them.

four noble truths. A fundamental doctrine of early Buddhism, it teaches that (1) all existence is marked by suffering; (2) suffering is caused by craving; (3) by doing away with craving one can gain release from suffering; (4) there is a method for achieving this goal. The method is that known as the eightfold path, which enjoins one to cultivate right views, right thinking, right speech, right action, right way of life, right endeavor, right mindfulness, and right meditation.

four unlimited kinds of knowledge. Unlimited powers of understanding and preaching that Buddhas and bodhisattvas possess. They are complete understanding of the Law; complete mastery of the meanings deriving from the Law; complete freedom in expressing the teachings in various languages and dialects; and the ability to preach to all people at will by employing the first three powers.

gandharva. A heavenly musician, one of the eight kinds of nonhuman beings who protect Buddhism.

garuda (garuḍa). In Indian mythology, a giant bird that is said to feed on dragons. One of the eight kinds of nonhuman beings who protect Buddhism.

gatha (gāthā). In Buddhist scriptures, a verse stating a Buddhist teaching or praising a Buddha or bodhisattva. Some sutras are made up entirely of such verses, while others have extensive verse sections, often restating the meaning of a preceding prose section.

Gaya (Gayā). City in present day Bihar. In Shakyamuni's time it was a city of the state of Magadha. Some seven miles south of the city is the site where Shakyamuni sat beneath the bodhi tree and gained enlightenment, at the place called Buddhagayā. Buddhagayā is sometimes referred to in Buddhist scriptures by the name Gaya.

Gayakashyapa (Gayākāśyapa). A disciple of Shakyamuni, a younger brother of Uruvilvakashyapa and Nadikashyapa. When his two brothers converted to Shakyamuni's teachings, he also converted along with his two hundred disciples.

Great Katyayana, *see* Mahakatyayana.

Great Maudgalyayana, *see* Maudgalyayana.

Great Vehicle, *see* Mahayana.

Gridhrakuta (Gṛdhrakūṭa). Mountain northeast of the city of Rajagriha where Shakyamuni is said to have preached the Lotus Sutra and other teachings. The name is often translated in English as Vulture Peak, but because Kumārajīva in his Chinese translation of the Lotus Sutra calls it Eagle Peak, that translation has been adopted here. It is also referred to as Holy Eagle Peak.

Hinayana (Hinayāna, Ch hsiao-ch'eng, J shōjō). The term *Hinayana* or "Lesser Vehicle" is used by followers of the Mahayana teachings to designate the other major branch of Buddhism. Hinayana teaches that, since Buddhahood is almost impossible to attain, one should aim for a "lesser" goal, that of arhat. It is the form of Buddhism that prevails today in Sri Lanka, Burma, Thailand, Cambodia, and Laos, where it is known as Theravāda or the Teaching of the Elders.

Holy Eagle Peak, *see* Gridhrakuta.

Indra, *see* Shakra Devanam Indra.

Jambudvipa (Jambudvīpa). The continent lying to the south of Mt. Sumeru, the "continent of the jambu trees." It is populated by people with bad karma, and hence Buddhism spreads there in order to bring them salvation.

Jambunada (Jambūnada) gold. Gold found in the river running through the forest of jambu trees in Jambudvipa.

kalavinka (kalaviṅka). A bird with a very melodious voice found in the valleys of the Himalayas.

kalpa. An extremely long period of time.

Katyayana, *see* Mahakatyayana

Kaundinya, *see* Ajnata Kaundinya

kimnara (kiṃnara). A type of heavenly being who excels in singing and dancing, one of the eight kinds of nonhuman beings who protect Buddhism.

kritya (kṛtya). A kind of demon.

kumbhanda (kumbhāṇḍa). A kind of evil spirit.

last five-hundred-year period. The first two five-hundred-year periods after the parinirvana of Shakyamuni constitute the era of the Correct Law. The

following two five-hundred-year periods constitute the period of the Counterfeit Law. The last or fifth five-hundred-year period marks the beginning of the
Latter Day of the Law, when the teachings of the Buddha lose their effective-
ness.

Latter Day of the Law (Ch mo-fa, J mappō). Third of the three periods which
the teachings of a Buddha pass through after his death. In this third and last
period, the teachings of the Buddha lose their power to lead people to enlightenment. It is said to last for ten thousand years or more.

Lesser Vehicle, *see* Hinayana.

level of no regression The stage one reaches in religious practice where one is
certain never to regress or backslide. In Sanskrit it is known as avivartika or
avaivartika.

Mahakashyapa (Mahākāśyapa). One of Shakyamuni's ten major disciples,
known as foremost in ascetic practice. After Shakyamuni's death, he became
head of the Order. The sixth chapter of the Lotus Sutra predicts that he will
in future become a Buddha named Light Bright.

Mahakatyayana (Mahākātyāyana). One of Shakyamuni's ten major disciples,
known as foremost in debate. He is also called simply Katyayana. The sixth
chapter of the Lotus Sutra predicts that he will become a Buddha named
Jambunada Gold Light.

Mahamaudgalyayana, *see* Maudgalyayana.

Mahaprajapati (Mahāprajāpatī). Also known as Gautamī. Younger sister of
Māyā, Shakyamuni's mother. When Māyā died shortly after Shakyamuni's
birth, Mahaprajapati raised him. Later she renounced secular life and became
the first nun to be admitted to the Buddhist Order. The thirteenth chapter of
the Lotus Sutra predicts that she will become a Buddha named Gladly Seen by
All Living Beings.

mahasattva (mahāsattva). A "great being," another term for a bodhisattva.

Mahayana (Mahāyāna, Ch ta-ch'eng, J daijō). One of the two main branches
of Buddhism. It calls itself Mahayana or the "Great Vehicle" because its
teachings enable all beings to attain Buddhahood. It lays particular emphasis
upon the bodhisattva, who vows to attain Buddhahood for himself and to
assist all others to do so. The Mahayana teachings arose around the 1st cen.
BCE and 1st cen. CE in India and spread to China, Tibet, Korea, Japan, and
Vietnam.

mahoraga. A being with the head of a snake, one of the eight kinds of nonhuman beings who protect Buddhism.

Maitreya. A bodhisattva, also called Ajita, who figures in chapter seventeen of the Lotus Sutra. It is said that he will succeed Shakyamuni as the Buddha of the future and that he will appear in this world 5,670 million years after Shakyamuni's death. Meanwhile he dwells in the Tushita heaven.

mandarava (māndārava) flower. Also called mandara (māndāra) flower. A kind of fragrant red flower that blooms in heaven.

mani (maṇi) jewel. A globe-shaped gem, said to be efficacious in warding off sickness and evil and in purifying water.

manjushaka (mañjūṣaka) flower. A species of white flower that blooms in heaven.

Manjushri (Mañjuśrī). A bodhisattva who plays an important role in the Lotus Sutra and other sutras. He is symbolic of the perfection of wisdom and is revered as chief of the bodhisattvas. In Buddhist art he is usually depicted riding a lion. In the twelfth chapter of the Lotus Sutra he is shown guiding the dragon king's daughter to enlightenment.

Many Treasures (Skt Prabhūtaratna, Ch To-pao, J Tahō). A Buddha who appears, seated inside the Treasure Tower, to bear witness to the truth of Shakyamuni's teachings in the Lotus Sutra. While still a bodhisattva, he vowed that, even after he had entered nirvana, he would appear and attest to the validity of the Lotus Sutra wherever anyone might preach it.

Maudgalyayana (Maudgalyāyana). One of Shakyamuni's ten major disciples, known as foremost in occult powers. The sixth chapter of the Lotus Sutra predicts that he will become a Buddha named Tamalapatra Sandalwood Fragrance.

Medicine King (Skt Bhaiṣajyarāja, Ch Yao-wang, J Yakuō). A bodhisattva who is the subject of chapter twenty-three of the Lotus Sutra.

men of lifelong wisdom. A term of respect for monks, indicating the lasting quality of their wisdom.

Nadikashyapa (Nadīkāśyapa). A disciple of Shakyamuni and one of the Kashyapa brothers.

Narayana (Nārāyaṇa). Another name for the god Vishnu in Indian mythology. Incorporated into Buddhism as a protective deity, he is represented in Buddhist scriptures as possessing great physical strength.

nayuta. A numerical unit, defined differently in different texts but clearly indicating an extremely large number.

nirvana (nirvāṇa). The word, which means "blown out," indicates the state in which one has escaped from the cycle of birth and death. In Mahayana Buddhism, it is taken to mean awakening to the true nature of phenomena, or the perfection of Buddha wisdom. In Hinayana teaching there are two types of nirvana. First is that of the arhat who has eliminated all illusions and will no longer be reborn in the six paths, but who still possesses a body. This is called the nirvana of remainder. Second is that which the arhat achieves at death, when both body and mind are extinguished. This is called the nirvana of no remainder or complete nirvana.

outflows. That which flows out ceaselessly from the six sense organs, that is, illusions. Outflows is another term for earthly desires. Hence to be free of outflows is to be without illusions or desires.

Papiyas (Pāpīyas). Another name for the Devil or Māra, a personification of evil.

paramita, *see* six paramitas.

parinirvana (parinirvāṇa). A term similar to nirvana, it is used in reference to the apparent passing away of the physical body of a Buddha.

Perceiver of the World's Sounds (Skt Avalokiteśvara, Ch Kuan-shih-yin or Kuan-yin, J Kanzeon or Kannon). A bodhisattva, the subject of chapter twenty-five of the Lotus Sutra, who assumes thirty-three different forms and manifests himself anywhere in the world to save people from danger and suffering. The bodhisattva was originally conceived of as a male figure, but in China and Japan frequently came to be depicted in female form and worshiped as a protector of women and children.

pishacha (piśāca). A kind of devil or goblin.

place of practice. The place where one carries out religious practice and gains enlightenment, often referring specifically to the place where Shakyamuni gained enlightenment.

pratyekabuddha. A "self-enlightened" being, one who has won an understanding of the truth through his or her own efforts but makes no effort to enlighten others.

Purna (Pūrṇa). Sometimes called Purna Maitrayaniputra (Maitrāyaṇīputra). One of Shakyamuni's ten major disciples, known as foremost in preaching the

Law. Chapter eight of the Lotus Sutra predicts that he will gain enlightenment as a Buddha named Law Bright.

putana (pūtana). A class of demons.

Rahula (Rāhula). The son of Shakyamuni and Yashodhara and later one of Shakyamuni's ten major disciples, known as foremost in inconspicuous practice. The ninth chapter of the Lotus Sutra predicts that he will become a Buddha named Stepping on Seven Treasure Flowers.

Rajagriha (Rājagṛha). Capital of the kingdom of Magadha in northeastern India.

rakshasa (rākṣasa). An evil or malignant demon who sometimes appears in Buddhist scriptures as a protector of Buddhism.

Saddharma-pundarika Sutra (Saddharma-puṇḍarīka Sūtra). "The Sutra of the Lotus of the Wonderful Law," the Sanskrit title of the Lotus Sutra.

Sagara (Sāgara). A dragon king whose daughter plays an important role in chapter twelve of the Lotus Sutra.

saha (sahā) world. Our present world, which is full of sufferings to be endured. The Sanskrit word saha means "endurance."

sakridagamin (sakṛdāgāmin). One of the four kinds of shravakas or voice-hearers. The sakridagamin is a voice-hearer who is destined to return to the world of human beings only once more.

sal tree. The sal or śāla grows in northern India, reaching a considerable height and bearing light yellow blossoms. Shakyamuni passed away in a grove of sal trees on the outskirts of Kushinagara.

samadhi (samādhi). A state of intense concentration of the mind, which produces a sense of inner serenity.

Samgha (Saṃgha). The Buddhist Order, one of the Three Treasures, the Buddha, the Dharma, and the Samgha.

samsara (saṃsāra). The ordinary world of suffering and cyclical birth and death.

samyak-sambuddha (samyak-saṃbuddha). A being "of right and universal knowledge," one of the ten epithets for a Buddha.

seven Buddhas. Shakyamuni and the six Buddhas who are said to have preceded him. The seven are Vipaśyin, Śikhin, Viśvabhū, Krakucchanda, Kanakamuni, Kāśyapa, and Śākyamuni.

seven treasures. Seven precious substances mentioned in the Buddhist scriptures. The list varies from text to text. In the Lotus Sutra the seven are gold, silver, lapis lazuli, seashell, agate, pearl, and carnelian.

Shakra Devanam Indra (Śakra Devānām Indra). Also called simply Shakra or Indra. Originally the god of thunder in Indian mythology, he was later incorporated into Buddhism as a protective deity.

Shakyamuni (Śākyamuni). The "Sage of the Shakyas," the historical founder of Buddhism. He is also known by his family name Gautama.

Shariputra (Śāriputra). One of Shakyamuni's ten major disciples, known as foremost in wisdom. The third chapter of the Lotus Sutra predicts that he will become a Buddha named Flower Glow.

Shikhin (Śikhin). One of the great Brahma kings.

shramana (śramaṇa). In India the word originally referred to any ascetic, recluse, or religious practitioner who has renounced the world in order to seek the way. Later it came to mean chiefly one who has renounced the world to practice Buddhism.

shramanera (śrāmaṇera). A male novice in the Buddhist Order who has vowed to uphold the ten precepts.

shravaka (śrāvaka). A "voice-hearer," that is, one who listens to the teachings of Shakyamuni Buddha. The term originally applied to Shakyamuni's immediate disciples, but later came to mean all those who follow the teachings of Hinayana Buddhism. The way of the shravaka constitutes one of the three vehicles. There are four kinds of voice-hearers: the srota-apanna, sakridagamin, anagamin, and arhat.

shunyata (śūnyatā). Emptiness or Void, the underlying reality that unites all being, according to the doctrine of nondualism in Mahayana Buddhism.

six faculties. The faculties of the six sense organs, the eyes, ears, nose, tongue, body, and mind.

six paramitas (pāramitās). Six practices required of Mahayana bodhisattvas in order to attain Buddhahood. The Sanskrit word paramita means "perfection" or "having reached the other shore," that is, having crossed over from the shore of delusion to that of enlightenment. The six practices are (1) almsgiving, which includes material almsgiving, almsgiving of the Law, and almsgiving of fearlessness; (2) keeping of the precepts; (3) forbearance or bearing up patiently under opposition and hardship; (4) assiduousness or diligence in practice; (5) meditation; and (6) wisdom. The Sanskrit names for the six paramitas are dāna, śīla, kṣānti, vīrya, dhyāna, and prajña. Sometimes four more are added, (7) skill in expedient means, (8) vows, (9) power, and (10) knowledge, to make ten paramitas.

six paths. The six realms or worlds in which unenlightened beings transmigrate. Counting up from the lowest level, they are (1) hell; (2) the realm of hungry spirits; (3) beasts; (4) asuras; (5) human beings; and (6) heavenly beings.

six transcendental powers. Powers which Buddhas, bodhisattvas, and arhats are said to possess. They are the power of being anywhere at will; power of seeing anything anywhere; power of hearing any sound anywhere; power of knowing the thoughts of all other minds; power of knowing past lives; and power of eradicating illusions.

srota-apanna (srota-āpanna). One of the four kinds of shravakas or voice-hearers. The srota-apanna is a voice-hearer who has entered the way to enlightenment.

stupa (stūpa). A shrine, usually dome-shaped, built to house the relics of Shakyamuni or other holy persons. The early Mahayana movement was said to have centered around the worship of such stupas or memorial towers housing Shakyamuni's relics.

Subhuti (Subhūti). One of Shakyamuni's ten major disciples, depicted in the Wisdom sutras as foremost in the understanding of nondualism. The sixth chapter of the Lotus Sutra predicts that he will become a Buddha named Rare Form.

Sumeru. A huge mountain that stands at the center of the world. The god Shakra or Indra resides on the top, while the Four Heavenly Kings live halfway down the four sides. At its base are four continents, the most important of which is that lying to the south called Jambudvipa, where Buddhism spreads.

Summit of Being heaven. Another name for the Akanishtha heaven, the highest heaven in the world of form.

sweet dew (Skt amṛta). In ancient Indian lore, a wonderful sweet nectar that makes the drinker an immortal. In the Mahayana sutras, the teachings of the Buddha are often likened to such sweet dew.

tala (tāla) tree. The palmyra tree or fan palm.

tamalapatra (tamālapatra). The leaf of the tamala, which is a kind of sandal-wood tree.

tathagata (tathāgata), *see* Thus Come One.

ten directions. Eight points of the compass, plus up and down.

ten epithets. Ten honorable titles for a Buddha; (1) Thus Come One; (2) worthy of offerings; (3) of right and universal knowledge; (4) perfect clarity and conduct; (5) well gone; (6) understanding the world; (7) unexcelled worthy; (8) trainer of people; (9) teacher of heavenly and human beings; (10) Buddha, World-Honored One.

ten powers. The powers of a Buddha, namely, the power of knowing what is true and what is not; power of knowing the karmic causality at work in the lives of all beings past, present and future; power of knowing all stages of concentration, emancipation and meditation; power of knowing the life-condition of all people; power of judging all people's understanding; power of discerning the superiority or inferiority of all people's capacity; power of knowing the effects of all people's actions; power of remembering past life-times; power of knowing when each person will be born and die and in what realm that person will be reborn; power of eradicating all illusions.

ten worlds. The ten paths or realms of existence in which all beings exist. In ascending order they are (1) hell; (2) realm of hungry spirits; (3) beasts; (4) asuras; (5) human beings; (6) heavenly beings or gods; (7) shravakas or voice-hearers; (8) pratyekabuddhas; (9) bodhisattvas; (10) Buddhas.

thirty-two features. Remarkable physical characteristics possessed by great beings such as Buddhas and wheel-turning kings. They are flat soles; markings of the wheel of the Law on the soles; long slender fingers; broad flat heels; webbed feet and hands; extremely flexible limbs; protuberant insteps; slender legs like those of a deer; hands that extend past the knees even when standing; concealed genitals; body height equal to armspan; body hair that turns upward; one hair growing from each pore; golden skin; light radiating from the body; thin pliant skin; well-developed muscles in hands, feet, shoulders, nape of neck; well-developed muscles below armpits; dignified torso like that of a lion; large straight body; substantial shoulders; forty teeth; even teeth; four white fangs; full cheeks like those of a lion; unexcelled sense of taste; long broad tongue; voice that can reach to the Brahma heaven; eyes the color of blue lotus blossoms; long eyelashes like those of a cow; protuberant knot of flesh like a topknot on crown of head; tuft of white hair between the eyebrows curling to the right.

thousand-millionfold world. A major world system in ancient Indian cosmology. A world consists of a Mt. Sumeru, its surrounding seas and mountains, heavenly bodies, etc., extending upward to the first meditation heaven in the world of form and downward to the circle of wind which forms the basis of a world. One thousand such worlds make up a minor world system, one thousand minor world systems constitute an intermediate world system, and one thousand intermediate world systems form a major world system. Therefore, one major world system comprises one billion worlds. There were thought to be countless major world systems in the universe.

three existences. The past, present, and future, or the entire span of time.

threefold world. The world of desire, the world of form, and the world of formlessness. The realms inhabited by unenlightened beings who transmigrate within the six paths. Beings in the world of desire are ruled by various desires. Those in the world of form have material form but no desires. Those in the world of formlessness are free from both desire and form.

three poisons. The fundamental evils inherent in life that give rise to human suffering, namely, greed, anger, and ignorance.

three storehouses. Another name for the Tripitaka, the three-part collection of the Buddhist scriptures. It is made up of the sutras, which contain the teachings of the Buddha; the vinayas, which deal with the rules of monastic discipline; and the abhidharmas, the treatises or commentaries on Buddhist doctrine.

three sufferings. Three types of suffering, namely, suffering that results from undesirable causes or conditions; suffering that results from the loss of something desirable; and suffering that results from the impermanence of phenomena.

three thousand worlds. Another name for a thousand-millionfold world.

Three Treasures. The three things that all Buddhists are enjoined to serve and revere, namely, the Buddha, the Law or Dharma, and the Samgha or Order.

three understandings. Three of the six transcendental powers: the power of seeing anything anywhere, the power of knowing past lives, and the power of eradicating illusions.

three vehicles. The path or career of the shravaka or voice-hearer; of the pratyekabuddha; and of the bodhisattva or Buddha.

Thus Come One (Skt tathāgata, Ch ju-lai, J nyorai). One of the ten epithets for a Buddha.

Trayastrimsha (Trāyastriṃśa) heaven. Heaven of the Thirty-Three Gods, second of the six heavens of the world of desire. It is located on a plateau at the top of Mt. Sumeru, where thirty-three gods, including Indra, live. Beings in this heaven have a life span of one thousand years, each day of which is equal to a hundred years in the saha world.

Tushita (Tuṣita) heaven. Heaven of Satisfaction, the fourth of the six heavens in the world of desire. It is said that bodhisattvas are reborn there just before their last rebirth in the world when they will attain Buddhahood. The future Buddha Maitreya is at present dwelling in the Tushita heaven.

twelve divisions of the sutras. Another name for the sutras or scriptures of Buddhism as a whole. The scriptures are classified into twelve categories on the basis of their style of exposition.

twelve-linked chain of causation. Also called the doctrine of dependent origination, an important part of the teaching of early Buddhism. It illustrates step by step the causal relationship between ignorance and suffering. It is described in chapter seven of the Lotus Sutra.

udumbara. A type of plant said to bloom only once in three thousand years. Used in Buddhist literature to symbolize the rarity of encountering a Buddha.

Universal Worthy (Skt Samantabhadra, Ch P'u-hsien, J Fugen). A bodhisattva who is the subject of chapter twenty-eight of the Lotus Sutra. He is symbolic of religious practice and is usually depicted riding a white elephant.

Uruvilvakashyapa (Uruvilvākāśyapa). A disciple of Shakyamuni, the eldest of the three Kashyapa brothers. When Shakyamuni came to Uruvilva village to preach, he became one of the Buddha's early converts along with his two brothers.

Vaidehi (Vaidehī). Wife of Bimbisāra, king of Magadha, and mother of Ajatashatru.

Vaishravana (Vaiśravaṇa). One of the Four Heavenly Kings, he watches over the north and listens to the Buddhist teachings, protecting the place where the Buddha expounds them.

Varanasi (Vārāṇasī). The capital of Kashi (Kāśī), one of the sixteen major states of ancient India. It corresponds to the present-day Benares. The Deer Park, where Shakyamuni preached his first sermon, was in Varanasi.

wheel-turning sage king (Skt cakravarti-rāja). An ideal ruler in Indian mythology. In Buddhism the wheel-turning kings are kings who rule by justice rather than force. They possess the thirty-two features and rule the four continents surrounding Mt. Sumeru.

wisdom embracing all species. Knowledge of the equality and differences that distinguish all things and phenomena.

Wise Kalpa. The present major kalpa in which we live. It is so called because it is said that a thousand Buddhas of great wisdom will appear in the course of it to save living beings.

World-Honored One. One of the ten epithets for a Buddha.

yaksha (yakṣa). A type of demon, one of the eight kinds of nonhuman beings who protect Buddhism.

Yashodhara (Yaśodharā). Wife of Shakyamuni and mother of Rahula. After Shakyamuni renounced secular life and gained enlightenment, he converted her to his teachings and she became a nun. The thirteenth chapter of the Lotus Sutra predicts that she will become a Buddha named Endowed with a Thousand Ten Thousand Glowing Marks.

yojana. A unit of measurement in ancient India, equal to the distance that the royal army could march in a day.

INDEX

OTHER WORKS IN THE COLUMBIA ASIAN STUDIES SERIES

TRANSLATIONS FROM THE ASIAN CLASSICS

The Lion's Roar of Queen Śrīmālā, tr. Alex and Hideko
  Wayman   1974
*Courtier and Commoner in Ancient China: Selections from
  the History of the Former Han by Pan Ku,* tr. Burton
  Watson. Also in paperback ed.   1974
Japanese Literature in Chinese, vol. 1: *Poetry and Prose in
  Chinese by Japanese Writers of the Early Period,* tr.
  Burton Watson   1975
Japanese Literature in Chinese, vol. 2: *Poetry and Prose in
  Chinese by Japanese Writers of the Later Period,* tr.
  Burton Watson   1976
Scripture of the Lotus Blossom of the Fine Dharma, tr.
  Leon Hurvitz. Also in paperback ed.   1976
Love Song of the Dark Lord: Jayadeva's Gītagovinda, tr.
  Barbara Stoler Miller. Also in paperback ed. Cloth ed.   1977;
  includes critical text of the Sanskrit.   rev. ed. 1997
Ryōkan: Zen Monk-Poet of Japan, tr. Burton Watson   1977
*Calming the Mind and Discerning the Real: From the Lam
  rim chen mo of Tsoṇ-kha-pa,* tr. Alex Wayman   1978
*The Hermit and the Love-Thief: Sanskrit Poems of
  Bhartrihari and Bilhaṇa,* tr. Barbara Stoler Miller   1978
The Lute: Kao Ming's P'i-p'a chi, tr. Jean Mulligan. Also in
  paperback ed.   1980
*A Chronicle of Gods and Sovereigns: Jinnō Shōtōki of
  Kitabatake Chikafusa,* tr. H. Paul Varley   1980
Among the Flowers: The Hua-chien chi, tr. Lois Fusek   1982
Grass Hill: Poems and Prose by the Japanese Monk Gensei,
  tr. Burton Watson   1983
*Doctors, Diviners, and Magicians of Ancient China:
  Biographies of Fang-shih,* tr. Kenneth J. DeWoskin. Also
  in paperback ed.   1983
Theater of Memory: The Plays of Kālidāsa, ed. Barbara
  Stoler Miller. Also in paperback ed.   1984
*The Columbia Book of Chinese Poetry: From Early Times
  to the Thirteenth Century,* ed. and tr. Burton Watson.
  Also in paperback ed.   1984
*Poems of Love and War: From the Eight Anthologies and
  the Ten Long Poems of Classical Tamil,* tr. A. K.
  Ramanujan. Also in paperback ed.   1985
The Bhagavad Gita: Krishna's Counsel in Time of War, tr.
  Barbara Stoler Miller   1986

The Columbia Book of Later Chinese Poetry, ed. and tr.
Jonathan Chaves. Also in paperback ed.   1986
*The Tso Chuan: Selections from China's Oldest Narrative
History*, tr. Burton Watson   1989
*Waiting for the Wind: Thirty-six Poets of Japan's Late
Medieval Age*, tr. Steven Carter   1989
Selected Writings of Nichiren, ed. Philip B. Yampolsky   1990
Saigyō, Poems of a Mountain Home, tr. Burton
Watson   1990
The Book of Lieh Tzu: A Classic of the Tao, tr. A. C.
Graham. Morningside ed.   1990
*The Tale of an Anklet: An Epic of South India—The
Cilappatikāram of Iḷaṅkā Aṭikaḷ*, tr. R. Parthasarathy   1993
Waiting for the Dawn: A Plan for the Prince, tr. and
introduction by Wm. Theodore de Bary   1993
*Yoshitsune and the Thousand Cherry Trees: A Masterpiece
of the Eighteenth-Century Japanese Puppet Theater*, tr.,
annotated, and with introduction by Stanleigh H. Jones,
Jr.   1993
The Lotus Sutra, tr. Burton Watson. Also in paperback ed. 1993
*The Classic of Changes: A New Translation of the I Ching
as Interpreted by Wang Bi*, tr. Richard John Lynn   1994
Beyond Spring: Tz'u Poems of the Sung Dynasty, tr. Julie
Landau   1994
The Columbia Anthology of Traditional Chinese Literature,
ed. Victor H. Mair   1994
Scenes for Mandarins: The Elite Theater of the Ming, tr.
Cyril Birch   1995
Letters of Nichiren, ed. Philip B. Yampolsky; tr. Burton
Watson et al.   1996
Unforgotten Dreams: Poems by the Zen Monk Shōtetsu, tr.
Steven D. Carter   1997
The Vimalakirti Sutra, tr. Burton Watson   1997
Japanese and Chinese Poems to Sing: The Wakan rōei shū,
tr. J. Thomas Rimer and Jonathan Chaves   1997
A Tower for the Summer Heat, Li Yu, tr. Patrick Hanan   1998
Traditional Japanese Theater: An Anthology of Plays,
Karen Brazell   1998
*The Original Analects: Sayings of Confucius and His
Successors (0479–149)*, E. Bruce Brooks and A. Taeko
Brooks   1998

A Syllabus of Japanese Civilization, by H. Paul Varley, 2d ed.	1972
An Introduction to Chinese Civilization, ed. John Meskill, with the assistance of J. Mason Gentzler	1973
An Introduction to Japanese Civilization, ed. Arthur E. Tiedemann	1974
Ukifune: Love in the Tale of Genji, ed. Andrew Pekarik	1982
The Pleasures of Japanese Literature, by Donald Keene	1988
A Guide to Oriental Classics, eds. Wm. Theodore de Bary and Ainslie T. Embree; 3d edition ed. Amy Vladeck Heinrich, 2 vols.	1989

INTRODUCTION TO ASIAN CIVILIZATIONS

Wm. Theodore de Bary, General Editor

Sources of Japanese Tradition, 1958; paperback ed., 2 vols., 1964. 2d ed., vol. 1, 2001, compiled by Wm. Theodore de Bary, Donald Keene, George Tanabe, and Paul Varley

Sources of Indian Tradition, 1958; paperback ed., 2 vols., 1964. 2d ed., 2 vols., 1988

Sources of Chinese Tradition, 1960, paperback ed., 2 vols., 1964. 2d ed., vol. 1, 1999, compiled by Wm. Theodore de Bary and Irene Bloom; vol. 2, 2000, compiled by Wm. Theodore de Bary and Richard Lufrano

Sources of Korean Tradition, 1997; 2 vols., vol. 1, 1997, compiled by Peter H. Lee and Wm. Theodore de Bary; vol. 2, 2001, compiled by Yŏngho Ch'oe, Peter H. Lee, and Wm. Theodore de Bary

NEO-CONFUCIAN STUDIES

Instructions for Practical Living and Other Neo-Confucian Writings by Wang Yang-ming, tr. Wing-tsit Chan	1963
Reflections on Things at Hand: The Neo-Confucian Anthology, comp. Chu Hsi and Lü Tsu-ch'ien, tr. Wing-tsit Chan	1967
Self and Society in Ming Thought, by Wm. Theodore de Bary and the Conference on Ming Thought. Also in paperback ed.	1970
The Unfolding of Neo-Confucianism, by Wm. Theodore de Bary and the Conference on Seventeenth-Century Chinese Thought. Also in paperback ed.	1975